Wall Street Journal Bestselling Author
ILSA MADDEN-MILLS

Christmas Cupid
Copyright © 2023 by Ilsa Madden-Mills
Cover Art: Sara Jane, AKA @IllustriousJane
Cover Designer: Letitia Hasser, RBA Designs

IMM Publishing

Copyright Law:

If you are reading this book and did not purchase it, this book has been pirated and you are stealing. Please delete it from your device and support the author by purchasing a legal copy. All rights reserved. Without limiting the rights under copyright reserved above, no part of this publication may be reproduced, stored in or introduced into a retrieval system, or transmitted in any form, or by any means (electronic, mechanical, photocopying, recording, or otherwise) without the prior written permission of the above copyright owner of this book or publisher.

NO AI TRAINING: Without in any way limiting the author's [and publisher's] exclusive rights under copyright, any use of this publication to "train" generative artificial intelligence (AI) technologies to generate text is expressly prohibited. The author reserves all rights to license uses of this work for generative AI training and development of machine learning language models.

This is a work of fiction. Names, characters, places, brands, media, and incidents are either the product of the author's imagination or are used fictitiously. The author acknowledges the trademarked statue and trademark owners of various products referenced in this work of fiction, which have been used without permission. The publication/use of these trademarks is not authorized, associated with, or sponsored by the trademark owners.

First Edition November 2023

88bee1be0e7f59b91ccf-f48a3d3d88625d7a351b57c28eaae8c124871b947dea

* * *

Also by Ilsa Madden-Mills

All books are standalone stories with brand new couples and are currently FREE in Kindle Unlimited.

Briarwood Academy Series

Very Bad Things

Very Wicked Beginnings

Very Wicked Things

Very Twisted Things

British Bad Boys Series

Dirty English

Filthy English

Spider

Waylon University Series

I Dare You

I Bet You

I Hate You

I Promise You

Hawthorne University Series

Boyfriend Bargain

Boyfriend Material

Stand-alones

Fake Fiancée

Dear Ava

The Revenge Pact

Christmas Cupid (Novella)

My Darling Bride (Dec. 2023)

The Game Changers Series

Not My Romeo

Not My Match

Strangers in Love Series

Beauty and the Baller

Princess and the Player

Co-Written books

The Last Guy (w/Tia Louise)

The Right Stud (w/Tia Louise)

Chapter 1

Iris

There are too many men in this place, and it stinks like beer and old grease.

Also...I don't think the bartender is very happy with me. Actually, based on the eye-daggers coming my way, I might as well have murdered Wayne Gretzky.

"If you want to watch the home shopping network," one of the men at the bar quips, "you should stay home. This is a sports bar, lady."

"My name is Iris," I say as I point a cheese stick at him. "There are fifty televisions in this place, all tuned to some sporting event. All I'm asking is if you can *please* turn this one to something worthwhile? I'm a paying customer too." I tilt my head at my glass of mediocre Chablis.

"There's a wine bar down the street, *Iris*," one of them calls out.

I flip him off, and they scoff. At least that's one way of ensuring none of them attempt to hit on me. I am *so* not in the mood to entertain gross pick-up lines from sports-obsessed goons.

Unfortunately, they don't change the channel, so I have to watch some former hockey pro squinting to read from the teleprompter, looking about as comfortable in his suit as I'd look in a bodycon dress. I munch on the fried cheese, savoring the melty texture as it hits my tongue. Yes, this place is awful, but I can't ding them for this tasty appetizer.

Someone turns up the volume, and I wince. Is it too much to ask for a bit of news, some culture? *Real Housewives* is preferable to this dumb blather.

Luckily, one of them looks over my head and says, "Holy hell, is that Slappy Miller?"

I spin on the barstool toward the door as the man in question comes in, brushing raindrops off his broad shoulders, only to be instantly swallowed by admirers. Not that it matters—he stands nearly seven feet tall, dwarfing them all. He's ruggedly handsome with auburn hair, a clipped cinnamon beard, and a bruise on his forehead the size of a walnut, the result of a throwdown at center ice during Thursday's matchup against the Rangers. The defenseman was a real prick, going for blood, so Slappy had every right to drop the gloves, much to my mom's horror.

Okay...I do know my way around a game. It's pretty much cardinal law growing up in the Miller household.

Eventually, the sea of admirers parts, and Nashville's favorite hockey player sidles up next to me, kissing my cheek as he leans in for a tight hug. I sigh inwardly. He feels so nice. I've missed him. "Hey, Iris."

"Impressive hat trick last game," I say loudly as I pull

back from him, enjoying the open-mouthed awe of the sports freaks around me. I do a little wave at one of them. *Yeah, I know the famous guy*, my eyes say gleefully.

"Eh, it was nothing."

I smile. He's humble, but he can't stop beaming in the afterglow of the Nashville Predators' latest win. Once again, he was MVP.

Grabbing my glass and the rest of the cheese sticks, I slip off the stool as his fans continue to gawk. "Really, Will? Was it too much to have dinner at a place where you're not a massive celebrity?"

He grins like the scoundrel he is. "Sorry, *Chez* Shitty Food didn't have any openings."

"They don't have bad food." I elbow him in the ribs as we go to a booth in the corner. He's always been a simple, burger-and-beer guy. "It's Chez Elise, anyway."

"Sorry to break it to you, sis, but I think I'd be recognized there, too."

I roll my eyes, but it's true. Due to a number of injuries this season with the Preds' first string, Will's been pulling double and triple duty. In this city, my older brother is quickly becoming legendary.

I have to say, I don't love it. I liked it better when I had him all to myself. "Don't let it go to your head."

"Who, me? Never." He slides into the booth, drums his hands on the table, and fastens his eyes on me as his smile fades. A serious look grows on his face. "We need to talk."

Oh, no. I groan and hang my head for a beat. I know where this is headed.

"Mom's worried about you." He pauses. "So am I."

"Me? Oh my god. What about you? You're the one

who's had two concussions and six broken teeth in two years."

He opens his mouth, baring yet another open space. "Seven. But I have good dental. Come on. You know Mom."

I do. She has lymphoma, in remission now. When she got the news a decade ago, we thought that was the end. Dad passed away when I was ten and Will was thirteen, so Mom has always worried about us being left alone. Will may face a pummeling every week on national television, but my mother's main concern has always been me. She thinks I'm the weaker child, the one who needs a little extra help in life.

It's absurd. I may not have a multi-million-dollar contract, but I have a stable job. I take my vitamins. I own a cool condo downtown. I have a good life.

"She's overreacting. I'm fine."

"No, you've been sad for a year. Liam broke your heart, and you haven't snapped out of it. You looked like a wilted flower this Thanksgiving."

"I'm no wilted anything," I insist, baring my own teeth this time. He growls back at me, and I pop him on the arm. He laughs—and that's the way our fights usually go.

"What are you doing for Christmas break?" He fastens an accusing eye on me. "You are taking a break, aren't you?"

I frown. "Yes..." Although not much of one. I like to bank my vacation days, save them for a rainy day, or a gorgeous guy who'll want to jet me off to the islands last minute.

Ha. I haven't taken off a single hour for *that*. I think I

have upwards of thirty days saved, but Will doesn't need to know that.

As if he can somehow sense it, he gives me a pitying look.

I let out an exasperated breath. "We're all spending Christmas Eve at Mom's, remember? Unless you want to uninvite me?"

"Of course not. But you should take some time off before the actual day. Learn to relax."

My lips twist. "What for?"

It comes out more sourly than I'd like, but I've grown to hate Christmas.

"Because 'tis the season, and you're going to Grinch it. I get why...but it's been a year. You have to get over it."

Last year, after three years together, I expected Liam would pop the question. Instead, he took me out to a romantic dinner two weeks before Christmas, only to tell me he was sleeping with his research assistant Kim Something or Another and wanted to marry *her*. I'd totally missed all the signs of a cheating boyfriend: his late nights, the missed calls and texts, the times when he said he was tired and wanted to sleep alone at his place.

"I'm over it, and I'm totally over the fact that most guys only date me because they want to get closer to you."

He tilts his head. "That's not true."

I give him a look. It's absolutely true. Liam always got tongue-tied around my brother. Whenever I wanted to go out, Liam would ask, "Is Will coming?" and get dolled up for *him*. Not a romantic thing, but definitely a thing. Ordinary men go absolutely bonkers at the thought of hanging with a pro sports player.

Will shrugs. "Okay, you're over it. But you still look stressed."

I cross my arms. "I love my job. I love my life. Everything is great!"

Again, he stares at me like I'm the pathetic runt of the litter left over at the pet store.

"At least I don't look like I had the crap beaten out of me."

"You *need* the crap beaten out of you. Maybe it'll wake your ass up," he says. "You're going through life like a zombie, just shuffling through." He gives me a soft poke on the nose. "I rented a cabin I can't use in the mountains. It's a couple of hours from here and I want you to go there, take some time off and relax, but I want you back at Mom's place Sunday night for Christmas Eve. I don't want you skipping out again, and that means I need you to stop bah-humbug-ing everywhere and be the jolly little elf I used to know."

He does have a point. I used to be Christmas crazy. I just don't know if I can ever get that girl back—that wide-eyed, joyful, un-jaded girl who loved Christmas more than anyone. I grew up, and growing up sometimes means pain.

The truth is, I've spent the majority of the last year in my pajamas, watching far too many reality dating shows, vaguely aware that life is passing me by. The only thing I've truly focused on is my job as a boot designer here in Nashville.

Out in the mountains, I could bring a pile of books, all my crafting supplies, and a bottle of wine, shut everything else out for a few days. Including people like my brother, who think I somehow need to be fixed.

"Really? So it's just going to sit vacant if I don't take it?"

He nods. "Yep. My agent says I've got to accept some award downtown instead, so you should take it."

"What makes you think I want to rough it?"

"It's not one of *those* cabins. It has all the modern amenities. Look." He pulls out his phone, scrolling through pictures of it.

Blue skies and puffy clouds drape over majestic mountains framed with pine trees and white laurel flowers. In the middle sits a rustic A-frame with a view of what must be a spectacular sunset. I scan the listing. Full kitchen with a gas stove. Giant stone fireplace. Adorable clawfoot bathtub. Views of the mountains out every window. I hold in a squeal when I see the phrase "premium hot tub".

My mind races, and something in my chest aches as I look at the photo. Of course, it was taken in the spring, and by now those mountains will be capped in snow or billowy smoke from the fog.

He thumbs something into his phone. "It's yours if you want, starting tomorrow. I'm texting you the address. Keys are in the mailbox."

"Can I bring Rob?"

"You mean Puck?" He rolls his eyes. "Yeah. Just make sure he does his thing outside."

"I will."

"You know I love the hell out of you, Iris. Forget the past. Look forward. That's always been our motto."

I blink rapidly at the soft tone. Will always has a way of knowing just what I need.

He leans in over the table. "Come on, sis, what's going on in that head of yours?"

"I'm thinking about how I adore you even if you're a bossy prick."

He laughs heartily as he tips back the beer the waiter brought him. "Bossy Prick—think I can get them to change my name from Slappy to that?"

I smirk. "Never. That's just for me and you."

"Am I the best brother ever? Like top tier? Like the most handsome, most kindhearted, most awesome person you know?"

I groan. "You're an asshole."

He snorts as we clink our glasses together.

After our food arrives, we dive into burgers and fries as he catches me up on his latest girlfriend, who apparently isn't going to last long, and I tell him about a pair of custom heart-themed cowboy boots I designed for a certain music star whose concerts have sold out all over the world. We fall into a comfortable rhythm, trading stories and cute insults as the tension of the day dissipates. We are inextricably connected, bound by a shared history of losing our dad young and fearing we'd lose our mother too.

I relax, my body shaking off the familiar heartache I've been carrying around since Liam dumped me, and when the bartender switches one of the televisions from old football games to HGTV, I nearly melt into a puddle of gooey happiness. It's going to be a great holiday.

Besides, what could go wrong on a little trip to a picturesque cabin in the mountains?

Chapter 2

Kyler

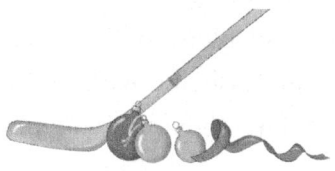

I live for pain.

A skate to the eye that needs 15 stitches. A toss against the boards that renders a man unconscious even before he hits the ice. A stick to the jaw resulting in spitting up blood for a week. *That* kind of pain, the kind that makes the crowd fall silent.

Not this crap.

I loosen my fingers on the steering wheel, trying to make my hand more relaxed, more comfortable, but there it is again: a dull throbbing, followed by pins and needles. It isn't long before I can't feel my fingers. I've only been in my offroad Benz for two hours since leaving Nashville, and the issue is back.

As I drive, I glance down at my hand. Looks perfect. The fans won't get it. There's a reason they call me the Beast. When I get knocked down, I get up again, covered in blood, every one of my wounds a badge of honor, and the fans love me for it.

But this injury? It's for sissies, invisible. I'm pissed at myself for letting it get to me. A pinched nerve in my wrist from a slapshot that went wide. I didn't even score. What a waste.

I toss a glance out at the passing mountain, eyeing the darkening clouds in the distance. The forecast isn't great with the possibility of blizzard-like conditions, but I'll be damned if I stay in Nashville with nothing to do but see happy people holiday shopping and having lunch with those they love.

I need distance. Like Antarctica distance. I need to get away from everyone who reminds me of what I've lost and what I just might lose.

With a sigh, I focus on the road as it winds up the mountain like a snake, the trees becoming sparser while still obscuring most of the view. In the gaps, the vastness of the mountain range stretches as far as the horizon, seemingly infinite in its size—a lot like my problems.

The vehicle lurches as I take a sharp turn, and the clouds in the sky darken even more, wind swirling around me. I press down on the gas pedal, feeling the need to get away from whatever is chasing me, even though I know it isn't anything physical. Maybe it's the uncertainty of the future, or this overwhelming loneliness, or the frustration of not being able to escape from my own thoughts no matter how hard I try.

Moments later, I pass a picturesque little village with artsy shops, small diners, and Victorian era lampposts. The town is decorated like it's Santa's North Pole with tinsel, lights, and Christmassy wreaths on every door. The streets are lined with plastic snowmen, elves, and candy canes.

Christmas Cupid

Twinkling snowflakes dangle from every light pole. I smirk, half expecting to see a reindeer ambling around.

It's mostly empty despite the cheery decor, probably because of the inclement weather. I watch as a lone man locks up a place that has outdoor snowmobiles, and I catch myself recalling riding one when I was a teenager in Vermont. Maybe the cabin will have one? I'd even take a sled. God, the thrill of riding snow down a big hill. Then I huff at my ridiculousness—I'm in no condition to put myself in a situation where I might get another injury.

I cruise past the town square and note a courthouse, but the thing that grabs my attention is an old Ferris wheel next to it. Not a big one, but it looks impressive. The lights on the wheel glow in the dimness of the evening, and the structure looks polished to a glistening sheen. *Welcome to Ferris, Tennessee, population 967* is lit up in the center of the wheel. I smirk. Yeah, this place seems a little too perky. I make a note to not come into town.

I leave the village behind, my mind numb. I don't even notice that I've reached the cutoff road to the cabin until I'm right in front of it. I'm just glad to have made it.

I park and stare out the windshield, watching the wipers move the clumps of snow that have started falling. My phone's sudden ringing interrupts the silence in the car, and I snatch it up with a familiar sense of dread. I take a deep breath before pressing the button on the dash to answer.

"Hey," I say, not disguising the apprehension in my voice.

"Hey," my agent Mike replies, his voice laced with concern. "You doing all right?"

I clench my hand into a fist before releasing it. "Yeah, fine. What'd they say?"

There's a pause before he speaks again, and the silence feels like an eternity. "It's not looking good, kid."

I inhale, trying to quell the rising panic inside me. I know I have to stay calm and focused on the task at hand, but it's hard when I'm faced with something that could potentially make or break my future. "What does that mean?"

"You know. You've had second and third opinions. You need the surgery. It can't wait."

"*After* the season."

"*Now*. If you wait, it's only going to get worse," Mike says, his tone hardening.

He's a tough agent who's been with me since the beginning. We don't see each other often since he lives in New York, but I can always guarantee he's got my back. This though?

"And by then, you might damage it so badly it *can't* be fixed at all. If you get it now, you'll be back on the ice this summer."

And I'll miss the rest of the season, the Preds' best season yet, in which Miller, Gibson, and I have been a well-oiled, history-making machine, the season we might finally get in spitting distance of the Cup. My hands tighten on the wheel. Over this sissy, nothing injury? This is like going off to war only to succumb to dysentery at basecamp. Worthless.

I don't speak.

"Kid, there's no debate. Either you get that surgery, or you're in breach of contract."

I picture him sitting in his downtown office, feet on his desk. Mike is the best in the business—if there were a trick to pull to put me back in play, he'd have already pulled it. I'm only one of his many pro athletes, a small fish in his pond, about to be a lot smaller.

I still don't speak.

Mike has never had trouble filling in silences. "Where you at, kid? You leave for Cabo with Gibson yet?"

"Not 'til Christmas Eve...Sunday afternoon. Right now, I'm in the mountains. Taking a few days."

"You should. I'll be in touch. Enjoy."

He ends the call without a goodbye.

Enjoy.

No. That's not what this trip is for. I won't enjoy a single damn moment of it.

This trip is about survival. As in, I'll probably kill myself if I have to warm the bench in Nashville for another game. I'm taking *this* trip because I need to get away from the fans. The other players. The media. For a few days, I won't have to fudge my way through the *When are the doctors going to give you a green light?* question.

And I'm going to use it to the best of my ability. I have two cases of beer and a few bottles of Jack in the back seat. I brought no luggage. What I'm going to do, while giving my right wrist a break, is exercise my left. I'm going to get drunk off my ass and act like a real mountain man who hates everybody.

Because right now, I do.

Then, I'll go to Cabo for Christmas and New Year's and live it up with my teammates, rejuvenated. That'll give my wrist a full two weeks to heal.

I'll be the Beast again, and I won't miss the most important season of my life.

I have to. I can't let my team down.

I step out of the car and inhale air scented with sharp pine and freshly cut wood, a combination that puts my teeth on edge, maybe because it reminds me of the things I don't have. I don't have anyone to celebrate Christmas with.

An owl hoots in the distance, and I glance around at the darkness. Best to get going instead of just standing here like an idiot. There's a red mailbox on the side of the road, the paint bright and cheery. I reach in and find a set of keys, just as promised. Then I park next to an attached garage. Several feet away and surrounded by trees is an A-frame log cabin. According to my buddy, it has all the modern amenities, but he didn't have to sell me on the idea.

All I care about is the privacy. I breathe in a lungful of cold air as the snow falls around me. I look like I'm in a fairytale setting, and if that's so, I must be the villain who's come to wreck it all.

The fingers of my right hand grow numb on the key I'm holding, reminding me of my worthless piece-of-crap hand.

I'm not going to let that be me.

I go to the back of the vehicle and open the back hatch. It's happy hour, all weekend long.

Chapter 3
Iris

"I hate you to the moon and back, Slappy Miller!" I growl up at the sky, smacking the top of the empty mailbox.

Tucked in his carrier, Rob, my French bulldog, looks up at me with unimpressed brown eyes. *Think you're overreacting, Mom?*

Yes, I am. I ease down to unlatch the carrier so Rob can exit, sniff at the snow on the ground, and take a little pee break.

I let out a long exhale. It's just that my goofball brother is *always* hatching plans that omit crucial details. My lips tighten, recalling the time he and his buddies invited me and my besties to a haunted house on Halloween out in the middle of nowhere. Turned out it was just an abandoned warehouse on the outskirts of Nashville and not a legit place where you pay a cover. As soon as we tiptoed through the broken doors, my brother and his buddies pulled out axes and chainsaws and chased us until we screamed and begged for them to stop. Yes, he is an adult, and his tools of torture weren't real, but he does like to play games with me.

Then there was the time I moved into my first apartment after college and he promised he'd help me set everything up because Mom was sick. I recall being excited at the prospect of meeting the friends he'd made on the Nashville Predators. Instead of brawny hockey studs who could carry all my stuff, my brother sent the guys from the city chess club to help. I huff at the memory. One of those guys was Liam, so really, it's my brother's fault I was in love with a no-good cheating doctor these past years.

After pawing a mittened hand over every inside surface of the rusting box, I decide my brother is full of crap. Unless...am I at the right house?

Looking up and down the road, I decide I have to be. This is 1246 Lovely Lane. There's another house down the way; I can't make much out, but there's definitely smoke coming from the chimney, and the lights are on.

My house is supposed to be blissfully empty for the weekend.

"Can I go now?" my young Uber driver says from inside her ancient Ford truck. "I hate driving in the snow. The roads get out of control up here."

I gnaw on my lip as I sweep Rob off the ground and into my arms. As much as I want her to stay with me, she reminds me of me in college, and I'd hate to be the one responsible if anything happened to her. "Sure. Sorry. Thanks for getting me here." If this isn't the right house, I can always trek to the neighbors and make some calls.

She simply cranks up the window and takes off, tires spinning in the snow, leaving me alone on a strange road.

Dammit, am I doing the right thing?

I survey the bags of groceries and suitcases at my feet. I'll have to make two, maybe three trips.

A cold wind whips at my puffer jacket as I hear the high-pitched, yippy howl of a coyote in the distance. A shiver washes over me, and I gulp. "I really hope this is the right place," I tell Rob, who just whimpers as if to say, *This is the way the Donner party started, Mom.* "Don't be like that," I chide. "I'm going to get us inside, somehow, and make some spiced cider. I'll even give you one of your cookies."

He cocks his head then barks.

"That's my boy." I ease him back to the snow. "Just follow me."

Grabbing a couple of bags, I trudge up the gravel driveway, catching a glimpse of the Smoky Mountains swaddled in cottony, low-hanging clouds. The house, too, is just as pictured—a well-maintained cherry-stained log cabin with a giant river-stone chimney splitting it in half. I get fluttery just looking at it. It's like a fairy tale, and I'm Goldilocks.

Now, if only I can get inside…

There's a dirt-covered Benz SUV parked in front of the detached garage. Must be the owners' spare vehicle, I suppose, a nice one. I climb the stone steps to the front door and knock, excitement dancing over me.

I count to ten, and when no one answers, I try again. Nothing. Obviously, there's no one in there.

"Just the two of us," I singsong to my dog as I push on

the door, not expecting much, but hurrah! It opens. "Ha! See, Rob? Our first spot of good luck."

Seeming unsure, he whimpers as I step in cautiously, aware that anything could be lurking in the shadows. The musty-smelling foyer is semi-dark with a single lamp lit inside the interior several feet away. Every step makes the floorboards creak beneath my feet, amplifying the quiet.

Uneasiness swims in my gut. "Um, it's nice. Isn't it?"

He growls low in his throat.

I put on a brave face for him. "Come on, let's explore."

I fumble around in the shadows, feeling my way toward the wall, my fingers grazing the rough-hewn wood. I turn on the overhead lights as I scan the space, revealing a simple yet beautiful living room with a sofa, a dusty piano in the corner, and an unlit fireplace with a carved mantle. Heavy pine beams crisscross the ceiling. Wow. So quaint. So perfect.

I jerk to a halt, balking at the deer heads on the wall, swallowing down a tingle of fear as I meet their eyes. They look macabre without their bodies! Rob looks up and trembles.

"It's okay, buddy. Don't make eye contact. Think about something else, like your wish list for Santa or the special little doggie treats I'm going to put in your stocking."

Overall, the room is small but cozy, and I especially love the yellow velour chair by the window. The fabric is warm beneath my hand as if someone just sat there recently, perhaps as they watched the snow fall. Of course there's no one here, so maybe the late afternoon sun warmed it up.

There's a small table next to it with a stack of books. I

thumb through them, shuddering upon seeing they're all Stephen King titles. *Carrie, The Shining, Misery.* Okay, it's cool. Sure, I hate scary stories, but hey, perhaps the owner is really into them. It doesn't mean he or she is going to show up and lock me in the cellar or anything. I push that thought away as I make my way toward the puffy navy sofa and test it out by plopping down on it. I exhale slowly. Yep, soft and cuddly, perfect for curling up and watching a movie.

Rob shivers.

"Don't worry, once I start the fireplace, it'll be warmer," I say, looking for the switch to light the fire.

No switch. It appears this fireplace isn't electric.

I check all the walls. "Is there a thermostat in here?"

Rob huffs as he gives me an unamused look. *Human problems, Mom. I need a treat. Give me one, please.*

There's no thermostat, and I groan when I see the stack of firewood and assortment of fireplace tools. Great. I might have to google how to start a fire.

"First, I want to see the kitchen."

It's small but efficient with wooden walls, weathered blue and yellow mosaic tiles, butcher block countertops, and pine cabinets. There's a small dining table in the corner with brightly colored mismatched chairs, the walls are painted a soft cream color, and there's a myriad of framed cross-stitches, most of them of roosters. A vintage vase with little cupids—or are they cherubs?—on it sits in the center of the table, filled with what looks like fresh pine tree branches. It smells delightful.

With just a glance, I can tell the kitchen seems well-stocked with everything I need, from a set of sharp knives to a collection of cast iron skillets. An old-fashioned gas stove rest regally in the corner, the wall behind it adorned with antique kitchen utensils: wooden spoons, rolling pins, and biscuit cutters. I clap when I see the island is covered with a variety of baked goods. My stomach rumbles at the tray of gingerbread men cookies and the loaf of banana bread. A welcome note is taped to the top of the island: *Enjoy your stay! -Ed and Riana, owners of Cupid's Cabin.*

Not a fan of the name, but I'm in heaven. I do a little twirl as I embrace the peace and quiet. No honking horns or sirens or pedestrians in the distance. Giddiness washes over me as I scurry around and grab a knife to cut a slice of the bread and pop it into my mouth. Earthy flavors of banana, sugar, and butter dance over my tongue. I moan around the texture.

"Oh God, this is so good, Rob. Yes, I'm having a mouthgasm."

He whines.

"Right—I haven't forgotten you. Your treats are still down by the road. I'll get them in a minute," I say as I check the stove. At least that works. The microwave lights up when I open it, too.

Grabbing a gingerbread man and taking a bite, I try the kitchen faucet, smiling when water comes out. Then I peer out the window as more snowflakes fall. "Oh, Rob, it's like a postcard here. This was the best idea."

Behind me, Rob lets out a sharp bark and scurries off down the hallway, his toenails tapping on the wood floor.

"Rob!" That's concerning. He only gets excited like that when there's something to chase. Hoping he hasn't found a mouse, I head after him toward the one open door, which is cracked enough that I can see a rose-colored braided rug and a four-poster bed.

Just what I need, a mouse in my *bedroom*.

Pushing the door open the rest of the way, I peer in. I saw this room in the photos. Victorian flowered bedspread, lots of dainty lace, hurricane lamps—the typical grandma room. As cozy as it looks, I frown.

Because Rob is nowhere in sight.

"Rob!" I whisper-shout, though I don't know why I'm whispering.

That's when I spot a sliver of light in the mirror across the room. A door is cracked open about an inch, and I hear the drip of water. The bathroom... Must be a leak, and I guess the owners left a light on in there.

Moving closer, I hear Rob yipping and scratching. Whatever he was after, he's found it. Expecting to see him toying with a poor, trapped rodent, I push the door open.

But it's not a mouse.

It's a very naked man, sprawled out in a clawfoot tub that's *way* too small for his burly form.

He practically a giant. Menacing scruff covers the lower half of his face, and there is a diagonal cut across his forehead, slashing from one temple to his eyebrow. The smell of whiskey wafts in the steamy room as cold brown eyes glare at me with murder.

So I do the only natural thing.

I throw my headless gingerbread man at him and scream.

Chapter 4

Kyler

I was just trying to fit my six-foot-seven frame into the dainty, not-made-for-a-man bathtub when it happened.

A dog the size of an oversized rat bolted into the bathroom and started yipping like hell at me, scratching at the ankle that wasn't in the tub as if he thought he could take me on. I've legit seen bigger cats around my house.

It *did* do something, though. I was so shocked I slipped on the surface of the tub and hit my head on the porcelain.

When I refocus a second later, it's not yipping I hear. It's screaming.

I crack an eye open to see a blonde in a high ponytail—two eyes, actually. Her mouth is open, her face is beet red, and she's looking everywhere but at me.

It's cute. *She's* cute. I take in the oval face that features fine creamy skin. She's wearing a flirty little black skirt and a black sweater with a pair of thigh high black boots. I linger on the fishnet hose.

Well, well. If I'd met her in a bar instead of here, I'd be all over that.

But this isn't a bar, I grouse inwardly as my anger stirs. This is the weekend I need to be spending *alone*.

With a disgruntled huff, she grabs a towel from the rack and slams it in my general direction, missing by a mile.

"What are you doing here?" she calls out as she puts her hands on her hips.

I pick up the gingerbread cookie she tossed at me. Someone's been eating my food. The cookie has soaked up water and dissolves right on my nipple. I flick it off as I glare at her.

"What the hell are *you* doing here?" I grumble, trying to bring my legs under my body and pull myself up so I can grab the towel lying on the floor between us. But the sides of the tub are wet and slick, and because of my hand, I can't feel the pressure enough to pull myself up. I try, only to fall back in, water splashing everywhere.

"Stop playing around. Use the towel for God's sake." She taps her boot as she gazes up at the ceiling.

I lift the towel, which has fallen into the tub and is now sopping. It's a freaking hand towel. Not going to do much good. "What do you expect me to use it for, sweetheart?"

I don't think she likes being called sweetheart, because her lips curl on one side as she snarls like a ferocious little fox. "Just put some clothes on and meet me outside."

Then she gathers the rat into her arms and sails out, slamming the door behind her. It vibrates on its hinges, and my mouth opens in twenty percent surprise, eighty percent anger. For a second, I just lie there, half-submerged in water, legs hanging over the rim.

What. The. Hell? I don't need this right now. I *really* don't need this.

I'm glad she's gone, because the way I get out of the tub is nothing like how I am on the ice. Taking a deep breath and praying I don't hit my head on the ceramic again, I manage to roll over on my knees and pull myself out. Jesus. I'm like a newborn. If I'd known there wasn't a shower at the cabin, I wouldn't have even come. Still grumbling under my breath, I find a towel that's only slightly bigger than the hand towel and sling it around my waist, leaving a big gap at my thigh, but whatever. She can deal.

I stalk out proudly to find her sitting on the bed, all prim and proper with her legs crossed. She's even slipped on a pair of sunglasses. At night!

She sniffs. "Oh my god. Put some clothes on."

Those sunglasses don't hide the blush that starts at her neck and rises all the way to her face.

I shrug. "Don't have any clothes."

Her lips puff out a breath of air, filled with disgust. "What? Are you like some kind of feral creature who just wandered in from your cave?"

I stiffen. Wait a minute. Back up. She looks like someone I know.

Why does she look familiar? Is she one of our groupies? Scratching my scruff, I try to picture her in gold and blue warpaint and a Preds jersey in the stands. Nope, not this snooty princess. I rack my brain, but the answer doesn't come.

I point down the hall. "They're in the wash."

She lets out a groan. Then she spins, manhandles the

quilt off the bed, and throws it at my face. "Put that on. You're embarrassing yourself."

"Nope. I'm not embarrassed. I feel pretty comfy."

"Just drape it over you. Please." She says the last word with a bit of begging, and well, I kind of like that, so I take the dainty flowered thing and put it around my shoulders like a cape. As I do, my towel falls off.

She picks that exact moment to slide her sunglasses down. More color hits her face as her throat moves. "Not like that," she cries out, hurriedly sliding her sunglasses back up to cover her eyes like that's gonna help.

"Then like what?" I take it off. "You want to dress me? Flowers aren't really my style."

She stands and stalks out of the room, her rat at her ankles. I arrange the quilt around myself like a long skirt and follow after her. Halfway down the hall, I stop at the dryer, pull out my still-slightly-damp jeans, and put them on.

When I get to the main living area, she's nowhere to be found. Maybe she left. The open front door says as much.

What, was she raised in a barn?

I go over to close it and wind up tripping over a duffel and a suitcase that doesn't belong to me. Does this mean she's coming back? Damn.

There's an ID tag on the suitcase. I flip it over and read it: *Iris Miller*.

I reel back. Oh, shit. This is Slappy's little sister.

I don't know her well, but I *do* know her. A couple of years ago on Halloween, Miller got a few of us together to scare the shit out of her and her friends at an abandoned warehouse. She was so pissed at him that she stormed off in a huff and I didn't get introduced. But last year, oh yeah, that's when we "connected". It was a New Year's Eve party at Slappy's place. Unease trickles over me. I recall being super drunk and a little lonely. I flirted with her and said something she didn't like, although I really don't remember what I said.

One look at my brawny frame and people know I'm used to throwing down, fielding some punches with heat, but she delivered a right hook to my face so hard I saw stars. So why is she here?

One answer springs to mind: This has Will Miller written all over it.

Slappy's the star and captain of our team, but he's not just that. He's the heart and soul of it, too. He does all sorts of things to boost our morale, usually in the form of a practical joke. One day at the beginning of the season, I arrived at the rink to find my entire locker filled with women's underwear. He once rode around on the Zamboni in nothing but chaps, pretending to lasso the players on the ice.

So that's what this must be, a practical joke. When he told me I could have this place because he couldn't use it, did he really think sending me his little sister was going to be funny?

For him, maybe. But me? What the hell am I going to do with *her*?

As I'm looking around for my phone so I can tear him a new one, I hear a scratching over at the door I just closed. Iris appears in the foyer, arms loaded with bags. She even has the strap of a bag in her *teeth*. There are snowflakes in her blonde hair, and I'd think she looks like an angel if it weren't for her eyes.

They're a gorgeous forest green, and they're screaming *You must die* at me. She clearly doesn't think this is funny, either.

A normal man would rush to help her, but I don't. Number one, I'm not sure what my hand will do if I put any pressure on it right now, and number two, she looks a little rabid.

Glaring, she slips past me and stomps to the kitchen where she deposits what looks like enough groceries for a week. She spits out the handle of the bag, and it plops on the island. "I don't know who you are, but I hate to inform you you're in the wrong place."

I sit down at the table and smirk. "I'm heartbroken you don't remember me."

She stares blankly, no recognition whatsoever. I wince at the ding to my ego. You'd think she'd remember.

Then she groans. "Oh, no...you're not one of *them*, are you?" Before I can ask her what she means, she puts her hand on her hips. "Ugh. Of course you are. I can tell by the muscles, the scars, the *everything* you got going on there. Perfect, just perfect," she grouses under her breath as she grabs a bottle of wine from the bag, twists off the top, and pours herself a large glass. And no, she doesn't appear to be about to offer me any. Then she looks up at the ceiling and growls, "I am so mad at you, Will!"

"Your brother."

She gives me a look that says, *Duh.*

I think she's getting the picture. "Did he tell you he wasn't going to use this place?"

She eyes me as she takes a sip of her red wine. "Yes, so I decided to come instead of him. But I was supposed to be *alone*."

My arms cross, and her eyes follow, widening at my naked chest. I smirk. "Same here."

"Well," she says, shrugging. "It's as simple as that."

"As what?"

She points at me with her index finger. "You have to go."

I let out a burst of laughter. "Not me."

She huffs. "Of course, you. Will's *my* brother."

"And so...?"

"So, I'm closer to him. I know him better. He's a nice guy, puts offers out into the world not thinking anyone will actually accept them. Kind of like saying 'We should hang out sometime' but not really meaning it. Sorry to break it to you, but he didn't expect you'd just show up here."

I hold up a finger, because I distinctly remember the conversation Slappy and I had over beers a few nights ago. He could see I was down. I couldn't tell him why, couldn't tell him I'm in danger of ruining our season. And yes, he's a nice guy, but he's a straight shooter. He's not a bullshit artist. He knew that what I needed was some time away from the real world. He knows I don't have any family close by to connect with over the holidays.

No one's going to be up there, he said. *You can do whatever the hell you feel like—away from all this.* Then I specifically recall him asking me if I was seeing anyone serious, and I laughed in his face. Sure, I've dated on and off, but no one wants to stick around with someone who's always on the road or at practice. I've learned to not expect much, to distance myself from getting close to girls so it doesn't bother me when they walk away.

I cock my head. "No...no...wait. How do you know he didn't tell you thinking *you'd* never take him up on it?"

"Because," she says, as if that's a legitimate reason. She makes a shooing motion at me. "You should go before the roads get any worse."

"Technically, I was here first." I rise up and ease over to her, casually reaching behind her to grab a piece of the banana bread she must have cut. I pop a piece in my mouth as I lean against the island. "Come on, sweetheart. I'm too pretty to throw out like dirty dish water."

She hoots. She actually hoots. "Hockey boys and their egos. You are pathetic."

"Like water off a duck. And you are a bratty princess. Tell me, did those boots slide in the snow? Did you bring any real shoes?"

"I can shove this boot up your ass."

I smile widely. Damn, I do like her spirit. She's a firecracker, but just as I'm thinking how cute she is again, her face hardens, and I blanch. She's seriously going to throw me out on my ass.

"Come on. It's a big place. We can stay together. Obviously, your brother trusts me. Perhaps he even sent us up here intentionally."

Based on the horror in her eyes, I might as well have suggested we share a toothbrush. Her hands tighten into fists.

"While I admit that does indeed sound like something my stupid brother would do, it's impossible. I don't know you. We've never even had a conversation."

It really hurts that she doesn't remember me. I smile, recalling the way she wrung my face with a slap that echoed in my ears. I was so shocked I fell back and landed on the floor.

"We're having one now." I try to go for another piece of bread, but she blocks me.

"That's mine."

"Seriously? Let me have one piece."

Her eyes narrow. "If you think you can take it, try."

"I'm not getting into a tussle with you just so you can run to Will and tell him I manhandled you. I'm not like that. Now, will you please move so I can have some of the bread?"

She shrugs. "Go on. Reach for it. But I'm not moving. You'll have to go around me."

Is she playing games with me? Is she gonna twist my arm when I get too close to her?

I really want that banana bread.

I kind of expect her to pounce on me as I slowly reach around, being careful not to brush up against her as I take another slice. Easing back with slow steps, I pop it in my mouth and chew. I expect the smell of the yummy goodness of bananas and walnuts to wash over me, but instead I get a nose full of her scent, citrusy with a hint of flowers.

She watches me chew, and I can only imagine the wheels turning in her head.

"Plus, it's a small cabin with one bedroom," she says. "I'm not staying here with some strange guy who could be a serial killer...or worse."

"I'm not a stranger, and I'm not a serial killer. I'm a hockey player."

"*That's* worse."

Okay, I'm sensing some serious hostility toward the sport. Odd considering her brother is probably one of the best players out there, but I'm also guessing from her sleek blonde hair and face full of makeup that she isn't much of a sporty girl herself. I bet she's always lived in his shadow and probably needs a therapist to help untangle those issues.

And yet she's the one looking at *me* like I'm insane?

"Just forget I said that, then. I'm your brother's friend."

She stares at me for a full ten seconds, squinting before saying, "Wait, wait. I do know you. You're...the one they call the Beast, right? A winger?"

I nod, proud my name has gotten around to even people like her who despise the game. That *almost* makes me a household name, not quite Slappy level, but close. Extending a hand to her, I try to bridge the distance. "Kyler Blanchette. Nice to—"

I stop with the pleasantries when she holds a hand up to silence me.

"Don't," she mutters. "I don't want to make friends. I just want you gone. How soon can you get your stuff together and get out?"

Anger brews in my gut. Screw this. I'd rather face the media's unforgiving firing squad than this. "Right now."

Stalking to the dryer, I grab my still-damp flannel and yank it on then shove my feet into my boots, grab my stash of whiskey from the pantry, and stomp to the front door.

I swing it open then stop. My eyes widen. Holy snow blizzard.

Those pretty snowflakes have nearly become a whiteout. The ground is covered with at least an inch or two of fresh snow.

"Are you going?" she says behind me, and the rat yips along with her, just as annoying as she is. "Because you're letting in the cold air."

I don't look back. Lifting the collar on my flannel, I head for my car. The ride back to civilization is going to be interesting, but it'll be better than spending my time with her.

Chapter 5

Iris

The wind ruffles his hair around like a Tasmanian devil before the door slams behind his broad back, and I wince. He didn't even put on a coat! What is wrong with him?

I groan as I run my hands over my face. My dear big bro thought this was funny. He's probably in Nashville, laughing his butt off right now. Did he even have an award to collect, or was that part of the ruse?

Gritting my teeth, I jab his name on my contacts list and bring my phone to my ear, ready to give him hell, but there's nothing. Dead air.

I look at the display. No bars. Great.

Stalking around the room, I search for reception somewhere, *anywhere*. Nothing.

Perfect.

I wind up at the front door, holding the phone up over my head as if that will help.

It doesn't.

As I'm posing like the Statue of Liberty in front of the door, I hear my unwanted guest revving his engine as he prepares to hightail it out of here. In the darkness and with no outside lights turned on, it's nearly impossible to see his car. Unfortunately, the snow doesn't help.

Good riddance.

For some reason though, Rob paws at the door, whimpering. *Why did you do that, Mom? It's going to be tough driving in this.*

"Oh, shush," I scold. "You didn't like him either."

Which isn't true. Rob likes everyone. Even people who call him a rat.

Fatal flaw.

"Besides," I say, more to myself than to my pup, as I look out the window. "It's better he goes now before it gets really bad."

Truth be told, it might already be really bad, but if my life is any proof...things can always get worse.

I don't know what my brother's deal is. After our conversation at the bar earlier, I almost think he *meant* to do this. He was clearly worried about my pathetic dating life since Liam, but did he really think the answer was setting me up with one of his hockey-obsessed teammates? Is he actually that insane? Did I not make myself clear to him?

Yep, Will's pretty much tops on Bad Boy Christmas List, right next to the Beast.

Okay, yes, Kyler Blanchette is ridiculously good-looking. Wavy mahogany hair, tall, rugged, the kind of man most women would just love to warm their bed. He's also got quite the body on him. I know this not just because he's an athlete, but because I can't seem to scrape the memory of it after our bathroom meeting. That sculpted chest, the cut abs, that V that leads to his hips...

Ahem. Doesn't matter. I know enough about him to be certain that while he may be every other woman's type, he's not mine. After all, at last year's New Year's Eve party, I did meet him. Awkward. I only went because I was feeling desperate after the breakup with Liam.

Big mistake.

Every topic of conversation, all night long, revolved around hockey. Everyone was drunk. It smelled like body odor and Gatorade Jell-O shots. I was in a bad mood from the get-go, so him sidling up to me with a lame pick-up line didn't help, maybe because I knew he once dumped one of my friends, Mara. Apparently, that's the type of guy you get at parties like that. I slapped him quite spectacularly, and he fell back, maybe in shock, then slid to the floor. I left right away.

So, I'm not quite sure what made Will think I'd be game for this little setup, if that's indeed what this is.

Not that I can ask him that. My phone's so dead I might as well bury it in the backyard.

Which is probably just as impossible as calling him, since—I stop, my eyes widening as I gaze out the window. There's got to be a good two inches of snow on the ground. When I walked in here earlier, there were only a few flakes in the air. Now, they're joining hands, having wild orgies in the darkening sky.

I peer down the driveway, squinting with my nose up against the cold glass, trying to see if he left. Moving to a different window in the corner of the house, I try to get a better view but still can't make out his black car.

Then I hear the sound, muffled by snowfall, of a vehicle letting out a dying gasp as if someone has stabbed it in the heart. *Grrrr. Grrrr.* Whatever that poor car's doing, it's not happy about it.

More whimpering comes from Rob as he scratches at the door like he has to use the bathroom.

Fine. "Don't go far. It's a whiteout out there. Just do it at the foot of the steps, okay."

He gives me what I think is a nod, so I open the door, and he bolts. No cavorting or bounding through the snow. He means business.

"Rob!" I shout, but he soon disappears in the curtain of white.

A blast of arctic air hits me at the same time, icy pellets of snow stinging my face. Ugh. There is no worse feeling in the world. This is why I live in Nashville and not Canada.

That fire is looking better and better. I still haven't had time to build it yet, nor will I have time if this crap keeps happening.

Sighing, I throw on my parka and step out. I do have stylish shoes on, but at least the heel is low. They immediately sink into the snow, and the exposed skin on my legs instantly starts to freeze.

By the time I take a second step toward wherever my silly mutt went, my skin is numb and burning. "Rob!"

But he's nowhere to be found.

Hanging on to the rail so I don't slip, I scuff down the

two steps of the deck. I whimper. What happened to my happy weekend of sipping wine in front of the fire?

A moment later, I hear a faraway yip coming from somewhere down the driveway. As I make my way through the snow, I realize that's where the revving car is, too. A few steps later, I see his Benz at the end of the driveway.

Oh, for god's sake. It hasn't even left the property. What is he waiting for, summer?

Then I realize its bumper is tilted at an awkward angle, and it's too close to one of the big pine trees for comfort. Looks like it slid off the driveway and into a drainage ditch.

Really? Aren't fancy SUVs supposed to hug the road like it's their best friend? Must be user error.

Nevertheless, the thing keeps revving, kicking up snow and doing absolutely no good whatsoever. I realize Rob's in front of it, supervising, yipping up a storm as if trying to give the idiot moral support.

A second later, the Benz lurches forward violently, gaining momentum. A little more juice and it'll be out.

My heart thumps. I see it happening in my mind's eye—the vehicle exploding forward, flattening my poor Rob, who happens to think he's a lot bigger and fiercer than he actually is. He'll be crushed.

I rush forward, oblivious to the searing pain in my feet. "Stop! Stop!"

He doesn't stop.

It's only when I lunge in front of the front bumper and scoop up my pup that the revving stops. I glare at the windshield, unable to see anything but the hulking outline of him beyond the snow-peppered glass.

He throws open the door. "What the hell do you think you're doing?"

My jaw drops. "You were going to kill my dog!"

"No, I wasn't!"

"Yes, you were!"

His eyes lower. "What? Is it stupid? It wouldn't know to get out of the way of a moving vehicle?"

Rob yelps a little, wiggling to get out of my arms. I expect he'll want to sic his murderer, but when I let him go, he simply climbs his boot and puts his paws on his jeans, looking for a pet. I huff. *Traitor.*

Will's jerky teammate just stares, stopping short of shaking him off. "I'm not having a really good day here," he mumbles, sounding about two seconds away from blowing his top.

"Hmm." I don't care.

"My vehicle slid into this ditch."

Duh. I can see that. I also don't care. I just want him gone. "All right. Well, see you."

I turn to leave, my teeth chattering.

"You're just going to let me freeze out here?" he calls after me.

"No. You almost had it before you nearly killed my dog," I tell him, blinking the snowflakes out of my eyes. God, it's cold. "Try again when we're out of the way. And then...have a nice trip."

"What? No, I didn't."

He's so infuriating. What made Will think...? "Yes, you did. I saw you!"

His jaw tightens. "I didn't *almost* have it. The thing's

stuck. It's not going anywhere without someone to pull it out. The ground is too slick and wet."

I stare at it, doubtful. I've never been mechanically inclined in the least, so this might not be part of his diabolical plan to spend the night with me. He could actually be telling the truth.

I shiver. "Where is your coat anyway? Who leaves for the mountains without a coat?"

"I forgot it," he snaps.

Right. Whatever. I need to get warm. As much as I'd love to sit out here and debate this, I think I'm getting frostbite on my toes. "Maybe the owner has coats here in the closets."

If his eyes were daggers, I'd be dead in the snow. "So that's it?"

I don't answer. I don't care if he has to hike down this mountain on foot. He can't stay here. That'll absolutely ruin everything.

But it is kind of cruel to just let him freeze. In that flannel lumberjack shirt, he might look like the mountain-man type who loves sub-zero temperatures, and I know he takes to the ice like a penguin, but this weather could last all night. I can't let him stay out here the whole time.

Maybe we can do that old sitcom episode thing where we use a line of tape to split the room in half and pretend the other doesn't exist. As I'm about to tell him that, Rob wriggles out of my arms, hits the powdery ground, and takes off in a flash. It happens so fast I'm not sure which way he went.

"Rob!" I shout, but he's gone. Crazy dog.

What is he chasing *now*? It's not my brother's teammate this time. Kyler is standing there, casually watching all this happen with his hands in his pockets and a smug look on his face.

"Sucks to be you," he says over the howling wind, and he goes back to his Benz.

Chapter 6

Kyler

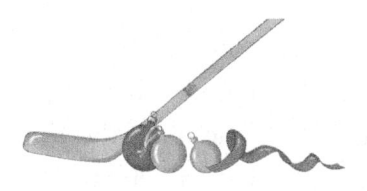

I get the feeling Slappy's sister isn't much of an outdoorsy girl. She's standing there stiffly as the snow falls on her head, her cheeks are rosy, and she's wearing those stupid boots. It's a wonder she doesn't fall to the ground and shatter like an icicle.

"Oh, no," she moans. "Rob, why did you have to run off in a storm."

I shield my eyes from the snow and search the trees. The rat is gone.

Not my circus, not my monkey. I trudge back to my car. There's no cell reception up here. I'm going to have to wait for someone with a tow to come along. If I'm going to spend the night in my car, fine. I have a full tank of gas, and at least I have Jack to keep me toasty.

You'll freeze, dumbass, I say to myself. Ugh. I've got to get back into her good graces. I crane my neck to peer between the trees. "He'll be back."

"No, he won't!" she says. "He's an idiot. He never does what I tell him to. He always does the opposite."

I raise an eyebrow. "Really?"

She nods.

Huh. I'm actually starting to like the rat now.

She lets out a groan of annoyance and stalks off in the direction her pet went. She only gets two steps before her feet fly out from under her and she goes sliding pathetically into the same ditch the back bumper of my car's caught in. She lets out a small shriek, and then, nothing.

I stalk over to peer down but can't see anything more than her once-bouncy ponytail. It's motionless, and she's oddly quiet.

It'll be just my luck if I killed Slappy's sister.

Walking back to the Jeep, I grab a flashlight, flick it on, and head back to the ditch. She's just sitting there, alive, knees pulled up to her chest.

"I really should have brought hiking boots," she declares mournfully. "I didn't even think to check the weather because I just thought I'd stay indoors and read and craft and cook and stuff."

I reach over. "Come on. Just get up."

She relents and takes my hand. I hope it's just the cold, but I don't feel hers in mine as I yank her up. It's not even pins and needles. It's *nothing*, as if it's not even attached to my body.

As I'm squeezing my hand into a fist, trying to get some —any—feeling into it, she lets out a big, drama-queen sigh.

I huff. Her dog's missing. She's cold. Boohoo. She'll be just fine in fifteen minutes.

Me, however? My condition could be permanent. Life altering. Life *ending*.

"Come on. Buck up. It's not the end of the world. Your dog will come back. He needs you to survive."

She gives me a pathetic look, tears in her eyes, and I must be a sucker because it melts something inside me.

"I-I was supposed to have a nice, relaxing weekend. Not this. I-I was gonna relax and take naps and get in the hot tub."

She sounds as miserable as I feel. Losing my mutt wouldn't be the end of *my* world, but it's clearly the end of *hers*.

I hate to admit it, but I get it. Misery loves company and all that. "All right, relax. Let's go inside and put better coats on and get another flashlight for you."

She nods and follows me as we trudge through the snow and back into the house. Opening the closet door in the hall, I pull out a heavy ski coat as I hear her rustling with her jacket. I frown when I see how thin it is. "Don't you have anything else?"

She waves a pair of fashionable red mittens at me. "These."

I heave out a sigh as I rummage through the closet, going through the owner's possessions. Finally, I find a bigger coat and a pair of snow gloves and toss them over my shoulder. "Put these on."

"Fine," she mumbles.

"And this too." I turn around with a thick gray scarf in my hands. It looks like it was knitted by hand and quite some time ago, but it will do. Without thinking, I march over and wrap it around her neck a couple of times then take her hands and push the gloves on to make sure they fit. They're a little big, but they're functional. "We'll get him back. What's his name again?"

"Rob."

Okay, not the name I'd give to a mutt like that, but sure. "Let's go," I say as I flick on the outdoor lights, thankful they illuminate the front and sides of the house. There's even a light over the garage that's currently pointing at my sad-looking sideways Benz. "Stay close to me. If you get lost, just look for the lights or tracks in the snow."

She nods and we head outside into the snow and wind, each of us with a flashlight. I cup my hands around my mouth and shout the dog's name so loud it echoes among the mountains.

Nothing. Not one yip.

I look at her. "He doesn't come when you call him? You get him obedience training?"

She gives me a sheepish look. "I've only had him six months. I was going to, and then—"

"Wait." I hold up a hand as something comes to me. No wonder the rat looked familiar; I saw it last summer in a pet carrier in the back seat of Slappy's truck. He brought the thing to the arena before practice, and all the guys gathered around it. Some of them wanted it to be the Preds' mascot. I told them if we wanted a mascot, it should be a man's dog.

Will said it was a gift for his sister. *She needs some cheering up*, he told us.

I didn't know why. Didn't care after that New Year's right hook, but now I'm wondering if there's more to this spoiled girl than meets the eye. Will might be a hell of a goofball, but he wouldn't have given her a puppy for a broken fingernail.

As I'm watching her, I realize the reason I was thrown off. Will had given it a different name. He called it...I can't remember.

"Hold up," I squint. "Will gave it to you, right? It wasn't always called that?"

She looks stricken. "What do you mean? He's always been my little Rob."

"Yeah, okay, but what else do you call it?"

Carefully, she says, "Mr. Squishypants? Robbie? My little Robin Redbreast? Robbie Dobbie Ding Dong? Robin Goodfellow?"

"Puck." I jab a forceful finger in the air as it comes to me. "He was named Puck. Like a hockey puck. Right?"

She glares at me. "Technically, yes, but I changed it. It didn't suit him. Besides, he likes—"

"Puck!" I shout, cupping my hands around my mouth again.

The name suits him because he's so hyper, bouncing off of every surface he touches. Puck *totally* suits him.

Faraway, there's a yip. Then another, coming closer.

I smirk at her. "Think he likes his original name. I mean, come on, what kind of name is Rob for a dog?"

She gives me a look of death then moves closer to the woods, trying to sight her pup. "Okay, *I* didn't like it," she mutters. "I do like Shakespeare, and *A Midsummer Night's Dream* is my favorite play. Rob is mischievous, like the wood sprite. I give my brother that."

I have no idea what drivel she's spouting. A puck is a

puck, not some wood sprite. The sooner we get the Puck back, the sooner I can get back to...living my miserable, lonely existence.

"Okay. Fine. Whatever. Here's what we do: I'll go around this side of the house, you go around the other, and we'll meet in the back. Don't wander off. Got it?"

"O-o-okay," she agrees, teeth chattering.

She has snot dripping off the end of her nose. No wonder Will gave her a puppy. As pathetic as she looks, I'd give her one, too.

"You know what? Scratch that. You go back to the house and get warm. I'll find him."

A small, grateful smile appears on her face. "Really?"

"Yeah. Scram."

The poor thing limps off toward the cabin. I head off in search of the rat.

"There!" she suddenly shouts, and it's like she's magically revived, because she runs off into the snow after her mutt. I hear it barking somewhere in the distance as she disappears among the trees near the back of the detached garage.

Then I hear her yell out in terror.

Chapter 7

Iris

They say in the moments before your death, your whole life flashes before your eyes.

That's not quite happening here. I can't breathe. I can't move. But I'm not seeing my favorite scenes of my childhood, either.

Nor am I doing anything useful, like thinking of the best way to survive this situation. Instead, my mind is focused on one word: *grizzly*.

The animal is sizing me up as if I'm its next meal. It's about the size of a big fluffy dog. Okay, so maybe it's a teenage grizzly, but it's standing between me and Rob, who's being stupidly brave and yipping at it like, *Come at me, bruh.*

Its head swivels between us, as if trying to decide which of us is the bigger threat. Then it rears up and paws at the air, like it's preparing to charge *me*.

My throat tightens in pure, primal terror. I never actually thought I'd see one this close. Like *really* close. Maybe it just wants to play?

Iris, get a grip. You are going to die!

My brain finally kicks in. They say to stay absolutely still, right? Say you shouldn't run because running makes you food? Well, that's great because my feet are not only frozen, but they're also rooted to the spot.

Other than Rob, who is doing a little jig, trying to get someone to notice him, everything is still. Even the falling snowflakes seem to have frozen in place.

Making no sudden movements, I glance side to side for an escape. The cabin must be behind me, but I'm too afraid to turn my head to look.

I flinch when the bear snarls at me. *Your move, dinner.*

Am I just supposed to stay frozen like this forever, until...what? He bites my head off? This doesn't feel like a standoff. It feels like the bear's playing with me. I briefly wonder if I'm one of those idiots who read I should stay absolutely still, thus making his job much easier.

He takes a step toward me, baring his jaws, showing sharp teeth glistening with saliva. I imagine them cutting into my flesh.

But then something happens. There's a loud bellow, like something Tarzan would let out before he rides in on his vine. The bear turns his head, and so do I, in time to see Kyler rushing forward with a baseball bat in hand. With his game face on, he looks like a warrior, his strides sure and fierce.

For a second, the bear just stares at him, unimpressed. But the second Kyler gets too close, it lets out a growl that makes Kyler's shout sound puny.

Kyler stops in his tracks. That determined look in his eye gives way to fear, right before he looks at me.

"Walk away slowly. Get in the cabin and shut the door," he tells me in a calm voice I can't wrap my head around.

I don't need to be told twice. With my heart pounding in my chest, I turn to the cabin and take giant steps. What about him though? I feel like a jerk for leaving him with a bear.

I duck behind a tree and peek out. Up on its hind legs, it's not as tall as Kyler, who's probably the tallest person I've ever met, and yet the bear makes him look tiny. It has claws. And teeth.

They're walking around each other like boxers in the ring, sizing each other up. Meanwhile, Rob yips at his heels, lending moral support.

"Rob!" I whisper-shout.

No good.

"Puck!"

The silly dog looks at me then runs over, jumping into my arms. I pet him, reluctantly, and only because he's warm and I'm shivering and need him to give *me* moral support.

The bear makes the first strike, but I don't have to worry. Kyler is as good at using the bat against the bear as he is with a hockey puck. The bear swipes at him, and he expertly wards off every blow. Eventually, the bear gives up, lets out an annoyed growl, and takes off in the snow.

All I can do is stare. That didn't really happen, did it?

Kyler lowers the bat and looks at his hand, flexing and unflexing it, a sour look on his face that makes me think he hurt himself. Then he plants the stick on the ground, leans on the top of it, and looks at me. "What part of 'get in the cabin' didn't you understand?"

I let out a breath. "I wasn't just going to leave you there to deal with a grizzly."

"Black."

"What?"

"There are only black bears in the Smokies, and he was probably just as scared of us as we are of him."

Well, isn't he a regular Davy Crockett? "Oh."

He picks up the bat and trudges through the snow past me. "Thanks for all your help."

I swallow thickly. He's only saying that because he thinks I should've said it to him. I was going to, but now…forget it.

I notice he's looking down at his hand, clenching and unclenching it.

"Hey, you were awesome. Truly. Thank you for your quick thinking. Where did you get the bat?"

"I keep one in my car for self-defense. You never know. I've experienced crazy anti-fans before."

"Oh. That sucks. Did you hurt your hand? I can take a look at it if you want."

He grunts. No? Yes? Can't tell. He's ahead of me now, and his strides are too long and the snow is deep. I fall behind, so I have to jog. Why won't he wait for me?

Whatever. I don't care. I may fall—in fact, considering how deep this snow is, I probably will—but not at his feet.

It's only when I've broken into a run that I realize something. I lost a boot somewhere between seeing the bear and now. It must have come unzipped and then slid

Christmas Cupid

off. With my adrenaline so nuts, I guess I didn't even notice.

"Wait," I say to him, letting Rob wiggle out of my arms and turning to look for it. I stoop over, feeling inside each footprint for it. Maybe it's already gotten covered in the snow.

Keeping a sharp eye on the edge of the trees to make sure the bear doesn't return; I check another set of prints in the trails. I groan. I'm pretty sure my toes are getting frostbite. Bending over to look at them, I brush the snow off, and...

My stomach pitches. Holy smokes. My pale-pink-painted toenails, once the same color as my skin, are now set against a canvas so purple it looks almost...dead.

My feet are dead.

"Ah!" I shout, just as Rob puts his paws on my arm and I go tottering forward. I almost land on my face but thankfully break the fall with my hands.

Turning over so I'm on my back, I lie in the snow, ready to accept defeat, to let the cold consume me.

Rob whimpers. *Uh, Mom? Are you alive?*

No. I am not. Snow falls right in my eye, and I whimper.

The next thing I know, Rob is standing over me, my boot in his mouth.

I smile with frozen lips. "I love you, baby."

Then another figure appears over me. The bear?

No, Kyler. He looks confused.

"What the hell are you doing? Now is not the time for snow angels."

"My feet are dead. I might need to have them amputated."

"Hmm. That sounds drastic, don't you think?" The snow crunches as he bends down and lifts my leg. I know this not because I can feel it, but because I see him do it. He pulls down the ankle socks I wore over my hose and carefully inspects them. He wiggles each toe like he's taking the piggies to market.

I'm too exhausted to complain.

He grunts. "They can be saved."

"But can I get off the ground? That's the question." I lurch up to sitting, and my head swims. My shoulders sway as nausea hits my stomach. "I'm gonna faint. We almost died," I say on a little wail as I wilt back into the snow.

"Your adrenaline is crashing."

The next thing I know, something burrows under my back, and I'm lifted up. Kyler scoops me into his arms and holds me up against his chest. It's so warm. And big. He's been out in the cold longer than I have, and yet he's radiating a pleasant heat. Despite my brain demanding otherwise, my body's instantly all in, snuggling up against his to absorb as much of the warmth as possible.

I wrap my arms around his neck so I won't fall, but after a few steps, it's clear he has this—I'm as light as a feather to him. I look up at his stubble-lined jaw and wonder if there's any angle I can view him that doesn't make him look handsome. Even with the telltale broken-nose divot along the bridge, he's sexy.

Hockey players. They can have everything wrong with them and still be so addictively gorgeous you can't tear your eyes away.

Christmas Cupid

"What happened to your forehead?"

"Yeah, banged it a while back. It looks bad but should heal up soon. Does it scare you?"

"No. Will is always looking like he got into a brawl and came out the loser."

"It's the hockey way of life," he says as I study the dusting of snow on his lush black eyelashes. His brown gaze flashes at me for a moment, and my heart skips a beat.

My throat tightens in refusal. Nope, not gonna go there. Do not get sucked in by his pretty irises. I manage to tear my glance away as he climbs the steps to the house.

"Out of my way, rat," he grumbles to Rob, who sits at the top stair, wagging his tail.

"Rob," I correct.

"Right, Puck."

I scowl at him.

He opens the door and walks to the sofa. If this were a romance movie, he'd lay me down and gently massage my tootsies. Instead, he plops me down so carelessly I nearly bounce off the cushions, then he stalks away as I'm trying to pull the pillow out from under me.

I catch him heading out the door. "Wait."

He turns.

"Where are you going?"

He points. "Outside. I recall seeing some wooden planks in the garage that might get me out of the snow. Then, I can get the hell out of here."

Regret washes over me. Even after saving me and Rob, he still can't wait to get away. I chew on my bottom lip. I was a little harsh, insisting he leave. This is not exactly the weekend of happiness I expected. I mean, I did want to be alone, but what if...

I imagine the owner of this place coming here and finding my calcified remains in this very same position.

"Well...you can wait until the snow lets up so you can call a tow tomorrow. If you w—" I stop as the feeling hits. It's like the pain of being drawn and quartered and beheaded all at once. "Ow! Ow! Ow!"

Moving around like a crab that's slowly dying, I reach under my leather skirt and drag down the fishnet hose then toss them to the floor. I grip my feet, trying to get the pain to stop.

He comes over and reaches over with his big paw to touch my foot, but I flinch away. The last thing I want is beautiful him touching my ugly feet again.

He holds up his hands in surrender then tosses me a wool blanket from the corner chair and goes to the fireplace. I recall thinking it'd take an act of Congress to light that thing, but he grabs the kindling and the wood and, in about two minutes, has a small fire going. He does some strategic poking with the fire tools, and by the time he puts the screen into place, it's grown to a bigger one.

With a happy grunt, Rob stretches out in front of the blaze and goes to sleep. Meanwhile, I've ventured a couple looks at my feet, which I've tucked under the cushion of the couch. Not only are they still screaming in pain, they're stoplight red. It's painful, and I writhe around, trying to find a more comfortable spot for them.

He sighs. "Okay, it'll get warm in here soon, and your toes will feel normal."

"It really hurts."

He knows better than to try to look at my feet again. Instead, he just walks to the door and goes outside. Guess that was one complaint too many.

I look around. Okay, so I got what I wanted. I'm alone. Great.

A moment later, the door opens again as Kyler hauls in a jug of whiskey. I noticed earlier that he brought nothing but alcohol for this entire weekend he expected to spend alone. I assume he planned to drink his time away.

I hear him rummaging around in the kitchen before sticking a glass under my nose. The smell of alcohol is so strong it makes my eyes water.

"Drink this."

"I don't drink hard liquor." It makes me way too chatty. And horny. Or I want to fight someone. Really, I'm sort of unpredictable.

He doesn't move it. "It's for the pain."

I wince into the amber liquid. "I brought some wine—"

"Drink."

His tone immediately makes me bite my tongue. Fine. I take it, dip my tongue in, and blink. Whoa. "Are you knocking me out so you can amputate? Am I going to wake up footless? And I spent $100 for this pedicure."

He doesn't even crack a smile. He's looking at me like I'm some pampered little woman.

Dude. It was a joke. But I guess he has every right to think that. Prada duffel and suitcase. Top-shelf makeup. Frou-frou dog. He doesn't know everything, though. I can party.

I toss back the drink.

He's watching me, so I smile, doing my best to disguise the fact that my esophagus has disintegrated.

"Want more?"

I nod since I no longer have vocal cords. In fact, I'm not sure I have a throat. Everything south of my chin is gone.

When he turns away to grab the bottle, I gag, my tongue hanging out, trying to fan air into my mouth. The second he turns back, I smile again as he refills my glass with the devil's liquid. I will never be able to drink a second one of that.

"Feel better?" he asks.

I shake my head. Except...when I look down at my feet, I realize they don't hurt as much. The first shot of alcohol has settled warm and happy in my stomach. It's kind of nice.

The fire crackles, spreading a warm orange light over the cozy cabin. Rob lets out a little snore, stretching. Actually, this *is* kind of nice.

I nod, pull the blanket up to my chin, and sip the Jack. This time, it doesn't burn at all.

"Magic Jack," I say as I stifle a giggle.

Chapter 8

Kyler

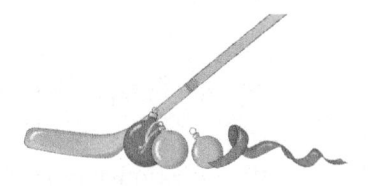

I think the princess is feeling no pain.

I can't complain. She's not forcing me to sleep out in my car, so I'll consider it a win.

She's flat on the couch, and her feet must be fine because she has them over the arm, wiggling her toes. She's giggling and talking nonsense about something with fringe on it. At first, I thought she was singing that song from *Oklahoma*—and really, she cannot carry a tune—but now I'm not sure. I don't think I could be any less interested, but she's going on and on, not even stopping to take a breath. She doesn't seem to notice the hollowness of the "uh-huhs" and "oh yeahs" I murmur every so often.

"I mean, really? Do you like fringe, Kyler?"

A rare silence follows. It's the first time she's said my name.

I was only half paying attention. I've ventured to the kitchen to find something to eat besides sweets. She brought a lot of weird food that requires preparation—salmon steaks, broccoli spears, edamame. What the hell's an edamame? Meanwhile, Puck's pawing at my pant leg, wanting something.

She asked me a question, one that requires a response.

I poke my head back into the living room. "Oh. Yeah. Sure."

She rears up on the couch, squinting at me with her brows furrowed. "You do?"

"Uh..." What was the question again? "No?"

She nods and gives me a thumbs-up. "That's what I was saying! It's so ugly! I hate it. Every single design, Bruce wants fringe this and fringe that. When I said it was too much, you'd have thought it was the end of the world. I told him, if we're going to be on the cutting edge with boots, we've got to think outside the box, do something different. You know?"

I cock my head, wondering which answer is more appropriate. "Uh-huh." Puck lets out a sharp whimper. "I think your rat wants dinner," I say.

She looks at him. "Oh, can you just open it for him? There's a bunch of packs in that grocery bag."

I grab the one I haven't looked through and find a small tub of food. Filet mignon, huh? The rat's eating better than we are.

I open it and set it down, and he licks my hand before diving in. Cute little bastard.

"You don't wear cowboy boots," she calls as I walk back into the living room and stand by the fire.

My lip curls. No, I do not. "The result of being from Vermont."

"Vermont?" She says it as if it's just recently joined the Union. "I didn't know that."

And why should she? Up until tonight, the only interaction we've had was that right hook. "Yep."

"Do you like it down here?"

I nod. "But I'm not the cowboy type."

"Hmm."

I huff out a laugh. My reply seems to disappoint her. I take it she likes the cowboy type.

I motion to her toes. "Are you sad your boot failed you in the snow?"

"Oh, forget that pair. I didn't design those. I got them at Neiman Marcus."

I stare at her, comprehension slowly trickling in. "You design cowboy boots?"

She glares at me. Clearly this is the wrong thing to say. And then I get the feeling all the fringe crap she was talking about two seconds ago might have pointed to the fact that she told me her entire life story. "I'm the head designer at Billie Kicks. I help with our line plus make custom boots for clients."

Billie Kicks sounds like the kind of boots no self-respecting northerner would ever wear.

"That's cool," I say as Puck comes back to chew on my pant leg. He's done with dinner. I nudge him off gently and gaze back over at the kitchen. "You have anything to eat for us?"

She squints at me narrowly as she hugs her glass of whiskey. "I'm not really hungry, but I have loads to eat."

"Yeah, I noticed, but is it edible? Not even one bag of Doritos?"

Fixing me with a look, she tosses her ponytail, which is currently on the side of her head. "And I thought you, as an athlete, would be into health. If it's not a holiday, Will eats like a saint."

I smirk. "I'm not a saint."

She's not impressed. "It's not my fault you don't know healthy food."

Nor do I want to. I really just want some chips and salsa right now. "Don't you have anything you don't have to *prepare*? You know, like snacks?"

"The edamame."

It takes me a while to understand that's how it's pronounced, the dried out green crap that looked like demented peas. "That's not a snack. It's alien food."

"It's a vegetable. It's delicious. And very filling." Her words kind of slur together, and I bite back a grin.

I grab the container from the kitchen and show it to her. "Looks sketchy to me."

She gestures for me to bring it over, pulls off the lid, and takes a bite. "Mmm."

As doubtful as I am that this vegetable can top a nice, crunchy chip baked with plenty of preservatives, I'll make that determination myself.

But as I reach in, she yanks the container away. "Mine." She shrugs at my scowl. "It's also not my fault all you brought this weekend was whiskey. You didn't plan very well."

True. I might not have done the most thorough job of packing, but I looked the place up on Google Maps and determined there was a convenience store a few miles away. Anything I had a hankering for, I assumed I'd be able to pick up there, but the snow has thrown a wrench in those plans. As if to remind me, at that moment, a mighty wind blows, shaking the house.

She giggles. "Did you bring *anything* besides alcohol?"

I look down at my jeans and flannel. No, I did not.

"I think my Jack has been *plenty* useful to you. Even more so than it was for me."

She looks at the half-empty glass wedged between her knees and sighs. "Fine. Try my snack for yourself."

I snatch a handful from the container and pop it in my mouth, chewing.

I barely stop my gag reflex. Nothing like a Dorito. Swallowing with some difficulty, I finally say, "Tastes like death."

She waves me off and pops another in her mouth. "More for me."

That's fine. I go to the window next to the reading chair and look out. Not only is the snow coming down fast and hard, the wind's picked up. Visibility was chancy outside before, but now it's nil. With the way it's piling up, I doubt anyone will be out on that main road tomorrow.

And that might screw up my Christmas in Cabo plans. I'm supposed to catch a flight from Nashville on Christmas Eve.

We might be stuck here for Christmas.

Nah, we'll get out.

Grabbing my phone, I take a look. No bars.

I wonder if Slappy planned this, the ultimate practical joke—stranding me here with his high-maintenance sister for the holidays. I let out a low growl. When I get back to civilization, I'm going to tear him a new one.

Pilfering through more of her groceries, I find some fancy sourdough bread and deli turkey. "She even brought Swiss cheese," I mutter as I make a sandwich then eat it quickly in the kitchen so she won't see me. I wash it down with one of the bottled waters the owner left in the fridge.

I laugh under my breath as I recall her facing off with the bear. I heard her muttering on the couch earlier about the "big grizzly" and how she nearly died. Black bears are normally very shy and avoid people, but they are still wild animals and therefore unpredictable. More than likely, Puck surprised him.

I head back into the living room and stretch my arms over my head. "Enjoy. I'm probably going to turn in."

She wrinkles her nose. "It's only eight."

"And I'm beat," I say, a euphemism for *I don't really want to spend the rest of tonight getting chewed out by you.* I take a step toward the bedroom.

"Wait! Where are you going?"

I turn to find her sitting up and staring at me in horror.

A slow smile curls my lips. Oh, I get it. One bedroom. "I'd sleep on the couch, but your highness's ass is currently on it."

She may not be an athlete, but she jumps off the couch with the agility of one. Guess her feet are better. "I'll take the bedroom. You can have the couch."

Thought so.

Stumbling a little, she puts her hand on the wall for support then disappears down the hall with Puck at her heels, and a moment later, the door shuts.

I inhale a long breath of air. Ah, peace and quiet. Here, in front of the fire, it's nice, toasty. I consider making a drink, but I'm too exhausted after the debacle in the bathtub, running my car into a ditch, and the standoff with the bear. Yet everything worked out. I'm here, and if I'm honest with myself, getting under Iris's skin today has made me a little happy.

"Best seat in the house," I murmur to myself, unbuttoning and shrugging off my shirt. I slide my jeans to my knees and pull them off. They're both dirty, streaked with mud from my jaunt outside. I'll need to wash them.

Tomorrow. I get the feeling I'm going to have plenty of time on my hands.

I hear the water running in the bathroom and picture her settling in for a nice long soak. She won't have to worry about me busting in on her. Nightmare scenario.

Several minutes later as I'm preparing to collapse onto the sofa, I hear the door creak open.

I'm covering myself with the blanket when she pokes her head out. "Um...I don't think the heat's working in the bedroom."

"Yeah, it is." I point to a propane heater in the hallway that I lit earlier. I'm sure it's what the owner uses at night, so it doesn't get cold when the fire dies down.

"It's freezing in there, though."

I stretch out on the sofa. "You have to leave the door open to let the heat get in."

"Ugh. They should have installed central heating."

"Uh-huh, but they didn't." I'm starting to pull the blanket up to my chin when she snatches it out of my hands. "What the—"

"I need—oh my god! Your penis! Why are you as naked as a jaybird?"

I stare at her in the flickering light from the fire. She has her hair up in some weird pink plastic pipe cleaner things, there's some white crap on her face, and she's wearing a big, fluffy robe that makes her look like a human marshmallow.

I sigh. "I can't sleep in clothes, even for you."

"Okay, but some underwear, *something*—"

"I go commando usually. I didn't bring any."

She gapes at me like I'm an idiot. "Whatever. Just—I don't want to see your hairy junk. Cover it up."

"What's on your face?" My heart did do a good hard thump when she appeared like that.

"It's anti-aging cream."

I snort. "How old are you?"

"Twenty-eight."

Same age as me. I don't think she needs that stuff, but girls are weird.

I point to her arms. "Blanket? Unless you're enjoying eyeballing my twig and berries."

Her eyes turn mischievous, and she gives me a smug smile. "Oh, no," she says in a baby voice. "Does the wittle bitty hockey player need his blankie?"

I grab a pillow and hold it over my pelvis. I mean, I have no issue with a girl checking me out, but this is Slappy's sister, plus my penis shriveled up the moment she appeared with curlers and cream. I can't have her thinking that's my true size.

I shrug. "Sweetheart, I only got the blanket to preserve

your innocence. I can lie here all day and night, naked and free as the wind. In three seconds, I'm going to remove this pillow. One, two—"

Muttering under her breath, she tosses the blanket to me, and it hits me in the face. After arranging it over my privates, I chuckle as I bend my elbow and prop my head up on my palm.

"You're a southern girl all right."

"So? Do you have a point?"

"What does 'naked as a jaybird' mean? Is that a real bird? Don't they have feathers?"

"It refers to a jailbird and how they take a shower when they get incarcerated. And I'm not sure it's just a southern thing."

"Oh, it is. *Y'all* southern people have some odd phrases."

"Oh, like Vermont isn't strange?" She huffs. "You call people who move into your state 'flatlanders.'"

I nod. "True, but we also have maple syrup, cider donuts, and apples. We were the first state to pass marriage equality. Can't top that. Go to bed, brat."

"Not a brat, asshole, I'm just having a very bad day," she snips.

I laugh as little sparks of anger seem to radiate around her. "Has the whiskey made you want to fight? Too bad. I'm tired and I've no time for a spoiled little girl."

"And you're a hockey jerk!" To punctuate her words, she storms down the hall and slams the door.

Ten minutes later, I haven't been able to sleep, probably from too much going on. I thought I'd have some time to decompress from the media and my injury, but someone has ruined it. I flick on the lamp and prop myself up on the couch as I crack open Stephen King's *Carrie*. I put it on the end table earlier.

Then I hear a door creak open slowly. A moment later, I'm quiet and not moving, wondering if there's a spooky spirit in the house when the sound comes again.

I nearly shout when she pokes her head around the hallway. The book goes flying and lands with a plonk on the ground. Jesus! Why is she sneaking up on me when I'm reading the master of horror?

"Um...you can sleep on the bed. It's too cold in there for me."

I glare at her. "You woke me up."

"No, you were reading. You practically threw the book at me. I said you could have the bed."

"I don't want it. I'm happy here."

I hear the floorboards shifting as she leaves then returns, dragging a quilt and a bunch of pillows with her. As she starts to set them up in front of the fire, she mutters, "Some luxury cabin..."

Without warning, Puck jumps on top of my center, like a brick to my groin. Talk about a wake-up call. I bend in half, muttering a curse as he makes himself comfortable at my feet.

Then I glare at the rat. "You happy?"

He gives me the same puppy-dog eyes he must've learned from the princess and lowers his head to snuggle against my leg.

Stretching back out again, I look over at her. She's curled up on the rug, wrapped like a burrito, eyes closed.

She's cute when she's quiet, even in those crazy-looking curlers.

"Good night," I tell her.

But all I get in return is a tiny, drunken snore.

Jack has performed its second magic trick of the night. It's finally shut her up.

Chapter 9

Iris

I awake, smiling, as pale light flickers through the windows in the cabin.

A long happy sigh comes from my chest, recalling the most awesome dream. I was at a Billie Kicks year-end gala and Bruce was giving me an award, telling a packed ballroom that they'd never use fringe again. Then he told me he was doubling my salary, and everyone applauded wildly, sending me and Rob floating on a cloud into the sky, maybe to Cowboy Boot Heaven.

When my eyes blink open, I see the white cloud. Then I realize it's snow, piled up, covering almost half of the window of this godforsaken *luxury* cabin, a dwelling that doesn't even have normal heat.

My eyes widen. Is God serious right now? That's got to be like four feet!

I throw off the blanket and am stumbling to the window to look at it when I smell something.

Food. *Burning* food. The air is hazy with smoke from burned eggs, toast, and...?

Spinning, I find nothing but a black cloud where the kitchen used to be. At that moment, footsteps come thundering in from the bedroom, and a voice growls, "Shit. Shit! *Shit!*"

I hear the clattering of something landing in the sink and the water running.

As the smoke clears, I find Kyler standing over the remains of what I can only assume was breakfast. Well, at least he's wearing a sweater now. It's faded and has a hole near the neck, and I can only assume he found it somewhere in the cabin. His hair is an unruly mess and is slightly damp as if he's bathed. The scruff on his jawline is heavier, accentuating his high cheekbones and square chin. I groan inwardly. He's still here. He's still devilishly handsome.

"Let me guess: those were my eggs?" I ask.

"Yeah. I just put the stove on and went to check on my clothes and—"

"And you nearly burned the whole cabin down?" I ask, incredulous.

He gives me an apologetic look. "Sorry. I was starving. I thought if I made you breakfast, you'd let me eat some of it." He points at a pot. "I did make coffee. The owners had a can. And I built the fire again."

Of course I'd let him eat. Does he think I'm a monster?

"Well, great, aren't you a regular Julia Child. You realize—"

"Hey, Casper, quit it. I said I'm sorry."

Casper? I've earned every one of the insults he's tossed at me, but what could he possibly mean by—?

At that moment, I wipe a stray lock of hair from my face, and something flakes off. Oh, my overnight cream that I never rubbed into my skin because I was a little tipsy. And I still have my heatless curlers in my hair, making me look like an old lady Shirley Temple.

I hold up a finger then run into the bathroom—it's still freaking freezing—and scrub my face then remove my curlers. I brush my teeth, apply moisturizer, and fluff my hair, and...better.

When I return to the kitchen, the smoke has dissipated. Slightly.

Taking inventory of the open carton on the counter and the package of bread, I determine he's wasted half of each. Considering the mess of snow we've got outside, I'm back to that image of the owner of this cabin finding our calcified remains. Well, unless our mountain man here can hunt better than he cooks.

My temper flares, but I suppress the urge to argue, only because he's wearing a truly sheepish expression. Not to mention, if I have to rely on him to kill my next meal, I'd better be on my best behavior.

I grimace. "How many times have you actually cooked breakfast?"

"Including this time? A few. I usually have a protein drink or cereal."

"The sugary kind? Froot Loops?"

"Cheerios."

"Hmm." At least he isn't a total child. I start to come around the counter and realize he is *not* actually wearing clothes. He's naked from the waist down, and I glare up at the ceiling, thanking God for big sweaters, though his is only partly obscuring his business. I point at him. "You're doing this on purpose!"

"Sorry." He grabs an apron from one of the drawers and wraps it around himself. "My jeans are still wet and in the dryer. My shirt too. They were dirty from yesterday—"

"Forget it," I snap, skirting as far as I can away from him and his dick. Even hidden by an apron—which has a giant rooster on it—I don't like that it's flying free. And truthfully, I saw a lot of his "area", and it looked pretty healthy and *big*. "Ahem. In the bedroom there's a bureau with some men's clothes in it. I saw a pair of jogging pants."

"Yeah, that's where I got this sweater." He grins. "Am I making you uncomfortable in my apron?"

I flick my eyes down at the cock that's hiding his "cock". I arch a brow. "I just don't want you to plant your naked bum on the kitchen chair when we have breakfast. That's gross."

"Aha, so you're going to cook us something?"

I nod. Anything to get some pants on him. "We'll do it together."

With a smirk on his face, he dips his head and bends his knees as he does a little curtsey, holding the edges of the apron out as if he's wearing a dress and bowing. "Yes, my lady. I will find some pants for you..." He does a spin to leave then turns back around so I don't see his butt. He calls out, "But I refuse to wear another man's underwear!"

I'm still giggling but stifle it when he comes out in a pair of gray joggers. I bite my lip when I see that they look like capri pants on him, the hem hitting just below his knee.

He slides in next to me at the island. "Show me how to cook, princess."

"Okay." He watches carefully while I crack several eggs into a bowl. "You did this part, right?"

"Sort of. I got plenty of shell in the bowl."

I add a little milk and start to whisk. "And this?"

He looks at me with confusion. I can just imagine what delicious breakfast I'd be eating right now if we hadn't had the four-alarm fire.

I hand him the fork. "Here. You try."

He takes the utensil from me and slowly starts to stir.

"No, whisk—like this." I take the fork back from him, and our fingers brush. A shower of sparks dances down my spine, and I shove them away as I show him once again. "It's all in the wrist, see? Makes the eggs fluffy."

This time, when I hand it back to him, he doesn't take it. Instead, he squeezes his hand into a fist. "Maybe you should do it."

Hmm, and I thought a hockey boy like him would excel at that.

Something comes to me. Didn't Will say someone on the team had a wrist injury? I'm never paying attention when the conversation turns to hockey.

I finish whisking and tell him to toast the bread. He manages that while I find another pan and start the eggs. I dig some butter and fruit salad out of the fridge, and voila. Breakfast is served.

We sit down at the round fruitwood table, surrounded on two corners by curio cabinets filled with knickknacks of little cupids, bears, and deer. I sip the coffee from a mug, not expecting much, but it's actually very good. "Mmm."

As he's shoveling down his food—he's halfway done before I even pick up my fork—he catches the surprise on my face and says, "It's good," as he shoves half a piece of toast in his mouth.

I dip my head to hide my smile. He's so different from my ex, who was all about manners and etiquette.

I look out the window and frown. I didn't think it was possible, but it's snowing harder. "There has to be several feet of snow on the ground."

"It's one for the record books." He stands up and goes to the window. "I should probably check the garage for some snow shovels. That way I can clear a path."

Hope ignites. "You think we can get out?"

"No, we can't go anywhere via car, but I should clear off the front steps and walkway so we can get outside at least."

I frown. "Why would we want to do that?"

"I don't know. You're all about health. I figure cabin fever, sitting inside for days probably isn't the best—"

"*Days?*" I shake my head. "I'm going to my mom's Christmas Eve."

He gives me a look like I'm crazy. "To be completely honest, I don't know if that's possible."

He's got to be joking.

"Ha-ha. You're funny."

He doesn't laugh.

I set my fork down. "What do you mean? Of course we'll be able to get out by Christmas Eve!"

He sits down and laces his fingers, a somber expression

on his face. "I was able to get a signal on the radio, and they said this is a historic storm. This area doesn't usually get snow this early, not this much of it, at least, and I haven't heard a single plow go by on that road out there. We could be snowed in."

I run my hands down my face. "There's got to be some way out! I'm not going to... What if you hike to that convenience store and call for help?"

"Me?"

"Well, I can't. I don't have the shoes," I explain.

He snorts. "You mean to tell me you brought that big suitcase with you, and you only have one pair of shoes?"

"No..." I look over at the boots from last night that I put near the fire to dry out. Besides those—which are ruined—I also have a pair of tan ballet flats and my velour, baby-blue Louboutin ankle booties, which look perfect with the new fuzzy blue chevron cashmere sweater I picked up from Bottega Veneta.

But I can't tell him that. He already thinks I'm a brainless, pampered princess. Sure, I love my fashion, but I'm also smart and savvy.

"Listen, sweetheart," he says, leaning an elbow on the table. "If I hike out, I ain't coming back for you. The only reason I haven't gone is because I doubt you would survive without my help."

My jaw drops. "Oh, yeah?"

He nods smugly, challenging me to come at him.

So I do. "Who's helpless? You can't even make eggs. And you would've starved to death by now if it wasn't for me, Mr. Can't-Pack-A-Bag-To-Save-His-Life!"

This isn't like me. I'm the collected one, the girl at

Billie Kicks who never shows a ripple, even when Fashion Week's upon us. But he's got me so worked up I'm ready to throw down.

Instead, he just smirks at me and points at my plate. "You going to eat that?"

I stare at him in shock, anger boiling over. "No..." I begin, confused as to why he's talking about food while I'm talking about a matter of life or death. If we don't get off this mountain soon, one of us is going to die.

But he doesn't even notice that I'm so pissed. This is why I hate hockey players—their smirky attitude, joking everything away, their oh-so-casual way of acting above it all, like nothing ever gets to them.

He casually takes the plate and drags it toward him, ready to dig in. Before he can, I latch my fingers onto the other side. "No."

He looks confused. "You just said..."

"No," I say again, more forcefully, pulling the plate back.

He's still pulling on his side and winning, so I yank it harder. He picks that moment to let go—probably on purpose—and the whole thing flies toward me, splattering into my face. Buttery bread. Eggs. Globs of fruit.

I stare at him in shock as it trickles down, some beneath the collar of my pajamas, the rest onto the floor, where Rob has a field day, eagerly eating up every last bit. *Thanks, Mom! This is very delicious!*

"Sorry," Kyler says, reaching forward to pat my face with a napkin. "I thought you—"

"Stop." I snatch the napkin from him as I stand up and wipe at myself, feeling sticky and gross. I know I went into this weekend hating Will, but right now I hate Kyler Blanchette even more. I need to get out of here, even if I have to hike the whole way myself.

As I start to head for the bathroom, he reaches out, grabs a piece of egg from the collar of my shirt, and shoves it between his lips. "Would've been better if you just let me eat it."

I'm considering jumping on him and smacking him around—just as someone knocks on the door.

Chapter 10

Kyler

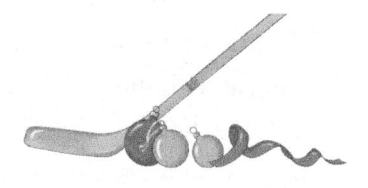

Right on time, there's a knock on the door. Good thing because I think she was about to deliver another right hook.

"Wonder who that could be," I say as the rat yips excitedly.

"Please let it be someone who can get us out of here before I go insane," she begs, clasping her hands in front of her.

I jog over to it as she picks up her robe from last night and puts it on as if she's afraid of being caught indisposed. She's not even showing a modest peek of skin. I don't know what her deal is. *I'm* the one she found mostly naked in the kitchen, plus I'm wearing someone else's too-tight jogging pants.

But when I open the door, the woman standing there doesn't seem to notice. Her smile widens. She has short, clipped silver hair, and oddly enough, the barrel-chested man standing behind her has an almost identical haircut and smile. They're also both wearing L.L. Bean parkas with fisherman sweaters peeking through the collars. With binoculars wrapped around their necks, they look like twins.

"Hi!" she says as I open the door, thrusting a stack of rectangular, foil-covered trays over to me. "We're Joan and Michael Davis. We live down the road east of you."

I remember the house with the chimney. "Hey—"

"Some weather we're having, huh?" the man interrupts, craning his neck to look inside. "It sure is cold out here. We'd love a quick visit."

Odd, but okay. They do have food.

I step aside to let them in. "I'm Kyler, and this is Iris. Come on—"

"Did you drive here?" Iris asks, practically jumping on the woman, just like the rat, who hasn't stopped yipping and bouncing since the knock. "Are the roads clear?"

She smiles, her round cheeks ruddy from the wind. "Oh, no," she says, pointing to her husband, who's still on the deck, trying to wrestle himself out of one of his snowshoes. "We love these winter hikes. Thought we'd take a little jaunt and see our new neighbors. When the weather's like this, it's like dressing the Smokies up for Christmas. I've never seen anything so beautiful."

Iris's shoulders slump as she grabs the dog protectively into her arms. He immediately stops barking, and she clears her throat. "Great to meet you. It must have been a hard trek to get here."

"No, it was a good workout," Joan replies. She points at her binoculars. "We saw you both arrive yesterday."

I blink. They were watching us?

"Do you have a truck?" Iris asks. She nods her head, along with giving me an accusing glance. "He drove his car into a ditch, and we need help pulling it out."

Michael comes into the foyer and shakes his head. "I don't think the roads are going to be clear for a while now. But you keep on keeping on, right?"

Joan laughs. "Last time we had a storm like this it was weeks before they could get to us."

Iris stands there frozen, so I play host. "Let me get you coffee." I glance at the dishes she gave me and smile. "What's this?"

"Oh, my famous hash brown casserole and some fried chicken tenders. Consider it an early present," she says.

Iris finally gets the picture and moves forward to take their coats.

"Just heat it up. Half an hour at three-fifty ought to do it," Joan says.

"We're not staying for Christmas," Iris says quickly, which has all eyes shooting to hers.

Michael makes himself at home at the kitchen table as if he's been here before. "I think Mother Nature has other plans, dear."

Joan pats Iris on the arm. "But don't worry. Michael here was in the Navy so we've traveled all over this planet, and I promise you, there isn't a better place to spend the holidays. Plus, if you need us, we're just down the road."

Iris pours coffee, looking at the woman like she sprouted horns. "I have to get to my mom's."

I nod. "And I have a flight to Cabo. The beach is waiting for me."

The two look at each other. "Oh, gracious," Joan says

in confusion. "You're spending the holiday apart? That doesn't seem very romantic. We assumed you guys were newlyweds."

I look over at Iris, who smiles uncomfortably as she sets the coffees in front of them. "Oh, he and I aren't together."

Michael strokes his chin, a mildly confused expression on his face. "You don't say. Well, what a surprise. This place is usually only rented to couples by the owners. It's called Cupid's Cabin for a reason."

"We don't need a cupid," I say sternly as I glance at Iris. "Right?"

She nods and rushes in to explain. "Yes, you see, he's one of my brother's friends. My brother rented this cabin and couldn't use it, so he asked if anyone else wanted it. We both took him up on the offer, not realizing..." She shrugs, misery on her face. "And then we got stuck here."

"Ah!" Joan grabs the sugar and adds several teaspoons full. Stirring it, she says, "Well, you make a very striking couple. Don't they, Mikey?"

He nods. "Absolutely. And you know, the good man upstairs works in mysterious ways."

I smirk at Iris and waggle my brows. *Hey, cutie.*

She just glares at me. "Yes, well, we're just trying to get back to civilization as quickly as possible."

"Aw, that's a shame," Joan says, sipping her coffee. "But if you do decide to make a holiday of it, Ed and Riana always kept an extra box of Christmas decorations in the attic. I'm sure they wouldn't mind you using them. We've known them for thirty years. They moved to Florida, but they send us Christmas cards. They miss this place."

Iris looks doubtful.

"I'm telling you, it's a very nice place to be caught, if you wanna be caught," Joan says on a laugh as she gives us both a knowing grin.

"I was nearly caught...by a bear," Iris says under her breath.

"You saw a bear?" Joan says, exchanging looks with her husband. "Did you shoot it?"

"No," I say. "I just scared it off."

"Aw, too bad. I'd get you a real good price if you wanted someone to stuff it."

"Stuff it?" I'm about to say this in horror, but Iris beats me to it.

Joan pats her hand. "Michael's little hobby is taxidermy. You should see our house—looks like the great outdoors. It's fine work."

Iris doesn't even try to hide the face she makes. She points into the living room where I spotted at least four deer heads on the wall. "You mean like the ones in there?"

Joan nods. "Yes, Mike did those deer. It's actually such a lovely way to memorialize an animal. They live on forever in your home. We have quite the collection at our cabin: raccoons, bobcats, bears, foxes, rabbits, even birds and ducks."

"You've stuffed a black bear before?" I ask.

Mike nods. "A couple of big ones and a cub."

What the devil? *A cub?* I'm angry but keep my face calm. A long silence prevails, but our guests are looking at one another, so they don't seem to realize Iris is turning green.

"You have any hobbies, Kyler, my boy?" Michael says, clapping me on the arm.

"I play a little hockey," I say, looking over at Iris, who's off in her own world, clearly still hung up on the baby bear comment. "And Iris here collects impractical shoes."

She glances up at me, already scowling as Michael says, "Hockey? I played a little myself, up in college at Syracuse. I still have my sweater."

"Don't let him fool you," Iris says, picking a glob of scrambled egg off the table and flicking it toward the sink. "Kyler doesn't *play a little hockey*. It's his life. He's a Predator."

"A Predator?" Joan asks in confusion.

Michael stares at me. He practically drops his full mug of coffee to the table, and it sloshes up over the sides. "Wait...you're number eight. Kyler Blanchette? The Beast?"

I nod, giving Iris a look. *Thanks.*

The until-now mild-mannered man lets out a long hoot. "Well, I'll be damned. We've got a celebrity here, Joanie!" He pats her hand and presents me to the unimpressed woman as if she didn't just hear the same information. "This guy's line of offense is one of the best in the history of the NHL. You, the Wizard, and Slappy Miller—wow. You're a force!"

There was a time when I loved this attention, milked it. Collected women's panties and men's assertions that I was more than a man, enjoying the compliments that inflated my ego. But that was a while ago, and now that I'm older, it doesn't feel the same. Since I've been off the ice and warming the bench for a full month...all of it falls flat, because I know what's coming next.

"Slappy's her brother," I point out, mostly to take the attention off me.

He glances at Iris. "Really?"

She pulls a face at me but manages to smile and nod.

He slams his fist on the table. "The Predators are my team. I've got to get you to sign something. You too, Slappy's sister." He points at me. "When are you getting back on the ice?"

There it is. The question.

I force a smile and shrug. "You got me. Got to work through a few things."

"That injury of yours is getting better, right?" He's looking at my hand.

I lower it to my lap. "Yeah. Won't be long."

"Good, good. Got to get your machine working again as soon as possible. You guys were killing it the first part of the season. I mean, your brother's playing some damn good hockey," he says, glancing at Iris, who's playing with a thread on her robe. "But he needs his right-hand man. We don't want to slip out of first place."

I rub my face, trying to think of a reply, but my stomach is churning too much at the thought of not being there for my team.

"Michael, darling," Joan says, leaning over and smiling at him. "I think these kids have probably had enough hockey talk. What do you say we be on our way?"

At least she can read the room. Still, they're pleasant, and judging by the delicious, aromatic smell wafting from the trays sitting on the counter, she's a good cook.

He stands. "Right, right. We'll leave you to it. But if

there's anything you need, anything at all, just let us know. We're right down the way."

After we both sign a notepad Joan had in her backpack, I walk them to the door, giving them each a firm handshake so they won't see how weak my wrist actually is. I hate disappointing fans. "Take it easy on the way back, and thanks for the food," I murmur.

"It was lovely meeting you," Joan says, and Iris nods a goodbye.

They step out the door, and I follow them onto the porch as they put their snowshoes back on. The snow's not letting up—another good inch has filled their footprints on the deck.

Looking out over the distance, I take a deep breath of the crisp, cold air. The snow blankets the mountain in a layer of pristine white. The sight is pretty, and for a moment, I feel transported back to my childhood in Vermont.

Growing up, snow was a constant. Every winter, we'd bundle up in our warmest clothes and head outside to have snowball fights and sled down the hills in our backyard. I remember the feeling of cold, wet mittens, and the taste of hot cocoa warming me up. My mom made the best cocoa, piled high with mini marshmallows and a sprinkle of cinnamon, her secret recipe. I went through her recipe box after she passed away and still have it at my condo, faded instructions written in her handwriting inside a little white box.

I remember how she'd wake up early on weekends to make breakfast while humming a tune, usually something from Madonna or Cyndi Lauper. The aroma of fresh blueberry pancakes and the sound of her singing would pull me out of bed. While my sister slept and my dad went to work, we'd sit at the kitchen table, devouring the pancakes and sipping on cocoa, giggling about hockey and my latest girlfriend.

My throat tightens, and it's hard to swallow. Jesus, I miss her. Dad as well, but we had a different kind of connection. He was a tall, burly man who worked late hours at his auto mechanic shop, and we bonded over sports, fast cars, and skiing.

I come back to the present as they call out another goodbye. Once they've gone down the hill toward their cabin, I walk back inside. Iris sits in the chair by the window, chewing on her lip as she gazes outside. She looks kind of sad and fragile, and I think I get it. She doesn't want to be referred to as Slappy's sister any more than I want to be reminded of my bum wrist.

Her blonde hair falls around her shoulders, the curls soft, and her mouth is lush, the bottom lip fuller, giving her a permanent pouty look. Funny how she looks nothing like Will. He's all muscle with a head full of wiry hair while she's petite with an angelic look about her—until she opens her mouth. I never thought I'd be into bratty girls, but...

Nah. I shut that thought down. I can't be attracted to Slappy's sister. She's a pain in the ass.

I want to say something to her, form a bond of solidarity, but instead, she just looks up and says, "They stuffed a baby bear. I'm really upset."

Her tenderhearted nature shows through.

I wince. "Well, we didn't get the whole story. Maybe they found it."

She huffs and pulls her robe around her neck. "I hope so."

I'm about to say something sweet like *Thank you for breakfast* or *I'm sorry you got food all over you*, but she stands up and stalks to the bedroom.

Chapter 11

Iris

The only good thing that's happened in the past hour is that Kyler finally put his jeans on. Other than that, things have gone from bad to worse.

The neighbors may have brought us food, but it's still blizzard-like conditions outside, and I left my favorite lip balm at home. At least I'm dressed warmly. Instead of my clothes, I found a pair of ski pants and an oversized black turtleneck sweater to match. It's not chic, but it's toasty.

My lovely companion, who is supposed to be rummaging around the house looking for supplies, keeps calling out in excitement with every ridiculous thing he finds in the attic.

"Hey! It's one of those ab roller things!" he yells as I use the mirror above the chest of drawers in the bedroom to apply my makeup. The bathroom is a little cramped on space on the vanity, and I wanted to be courteous and leave room for Kyler's bag of toiletries. Thank goodness he only brought deodorant and soap.

"Hell, these VHS tapes are ancient. I've never heard of most of these titles—oh wait, here's *Titanic*. I've never seen it, but chicks love it," he calls out from above me.

I roll my eyes. "Spoiler alert: Jack dies in the end!"

He cries out in glee, clearly not caring about *Titanic*. "An electric apple peeler! Totally sealed and unopened! Did you bring any apples?"

"No," I say as I move to glance up at where I can see him as he leans down and pokes his head into the opening to the walk-up attic. Wearing a stupid grin, he waves the box at me, and I grimace. "I really only care if you found a magic device that can teleport me off this mountain."

"I feel you, Iris," he replies, his eyes meeting mine, and I blink, realizing it's the first time he's called me by my name. Ugh, I hate how the sound of it drips like honey from his tongue.

"Wish we had apples." He gives the peeler box a look then tosses it somewhere inside the attic. He comes down the ladder, wiping the dust from his hands as he follows me into the bedroom and leans against the door jamb. I apply primer to my skin then add some tinted foundation with sunscreen. Normally, I'd never let a man watch me apply makeup, but I figure he and I will never see each other again.

He brushes those brandy-colored eyes over my attire, seeming to approve. "Also didn't find any Christmas decorations."

I am not decorating this place and settling in. That's like admitting defeat. "We don't need Christmas decorations. We need to find a way out of here."

He shrugs broad shoulders, the flannel material

stretching over his sculpted arms as he crosses them. I try not to watch how fluid his movements are.

"I don't know. Maybe instead of busting our asses on what's not going to happen, we should make the best of it. Could cheer us up to decorate a little. This kind of reminds me of our Christmases back home when I was growing up."

"If you long for an old-fashioned snowbound Christmas so much, why are you going to Cabo?"

"That was the Wizard's idea."

I make a face. "Will didn't want to go. He says Christmas is the only time palm trees are depressing."

He nods. "It's not like I can go back to Vermont."

"Your parents aren't there?"

"They passed away in a car accident several years ago. I finally sold their house a few months back. I hung on to it for a long time but realized they aren't really there anymore." His voice doesn't sound sad, but there's a furrow on his brow and his lips are downturned.

I sympathize with him so much I want to hug him. "And you don't have siblings or family or, um..." a girlfriend?

He rakes a hand through his curls, looking away from me as if to hide his face. "I have a sister and a couple of teenage nieces in California. They have their own thing going on with her husband's family, so I usually just send them gifts. Which reminds me, I haven't done that yet. Anyway, Cabo was my best option."

No wonder he doesn't seem so banged up about missing the holiday. "I've spent Christmas with my mom and brother since I was a baby. And my dad, but he died when I was small. It's an even more important tradition now, for the three of us. I really can't miss it this year."

"I know."

I give him a look. How could he?

He clears his throat. "Your brother told me about the tradition. How after your dad died, it was always the three of you, together in your mom's house, singing Christmas carols and stuff."

Just the thought of it warms me. My mother has a little Italian in her, so she always makes the seven fishes. Usually the good stuff, like fried calamari and shrimp scampi, but sometimes she experiments with eel and other weird things. Then, we have to wait until midnight before we open presents, so we sit around the fire in our matching pajamas, singing Christmas carols as badly as possible. It's always been my favorite night of the year.

It became an even bigger deal after my mother was diagnosed with cancer right before Christmas, and Will and I talked about how to make it special. We said since it could be the last Christmas with the three of us together, we had to make it something to treasure.

And we did.

A scare like that does that. We were always thinking, *This could be our last Christmas together* and really doing it up—more decorations, more carols, more food, more ugly Christmas sweaters, more everything. Each one was bigger and more obnoxious and more memorable than the last.

My smile fades as I remember last year. I was so excited to introduce Liam to the tradition. I was going to make our group of three into four. I blabbed on and on about how Liam would fit right in.

Little did I know about him and Assistant Kim. Liam didn't just ruin my Christmas; he ruined my mother's and Will's, because they were too worried about me to enjoy it. He marred our family tradition. I'm the idiot who let him do it.

"Are you going to have it at Will's place? He just closed on that big house in Franklin a few weeks ago."

I shake my head. I haven't even been there, but he's shown me pictures. It's a $3 million mansion with all the space to spread out...and he's the only one living there. But with his NHL contract, it's a drop in the bucket. He joked it was *to impress the ladies*, like he needs any help doing that.

Kyler, too, has never had any trouble.

"No. It's always at my mom's. I was caught up in getting a pair of custom boots designed and haven't had a chance drive out there. Have you been?"

He nods. "It has an ice rink. It's pretty cool. I'm thinking of building in the same neighborhood. It will be nice to be able to see him off the ice too."

Something gets stuck in my throat. More empathy. Kyler likes Will a lot and vice versa. He doesn't have any family around, and maybe Will *is* his family.

I stop applying mascara as tears unexpectedly spring to my eyes.

He notices, his tone soft. "Hey, you okay?"

I squeeze them back. "Yeah. Yeah, sure. I just know my mom and Will are going to be really bent out of shape if I'm not there this year." I pull my hair back into a high ponytail. "I want to look in the garage. There might be a snowmobile or a truck in there."

"I was going to look there next…" he says, although I think he was just planning to look for those decorations. "Why are you doing that, then?"

"What?"

"Putting that shit on your face?"

Oh. I laugh. "Force of habit? I never go out without a little makeup."

"Even to the garage?"

I hold up a hand. "You worry about your life, and I'll worry about mine."

"I'm just saying, you're pretty. Sorta. Maybe. For a bratty princess."

My heart skips a beat.

I throw my mascara wand in my bag, and he gives me that smirk again. He loves getting to me, doesn't he? The obvious move would be not to show a ripple, but he makes it absolutely impossible. So why do I like it?

I don't!

I stalk past him, stepping into the ruined boots from last night. Throwing on my jacket and the scarf from the closet, I head for the door. He doesn't follow. I was kind of hoping he would because I don't actually know how to work a snowmobile if I did stumble upon one, and I'm sure Mr. Vermont was probably born on one.

I look back. "You can come, or not…" And give him sufficient time to join me.

When I see him getting into his coat and boots, I smile then open the door. I wish I could say the going is easy, but I don't get two steps before I'm frozen. Not only is the snow coming down sideways and attacking my face, but the wind is also so cold all the layers do nothing. I might as well be naked, not to mention my feet keep sinking into snow that's up to my thigh.

A moment later, Kyler comes out behind me and, in two seconds, barrels in front of me as if this is just a stroll to him. When he reaches the garage door that is pulled down, he uses his set of keys to unlock it, pushes it open, and looks back at me.

When I finally get there (about an hour later), he smirks. "Take your time."

When I shake off the snow from my hair, I'm sure to fling it in his direction, not that he minds. He simply laughs.

It only takes a glance around to determine there is no vehicle of any sort in this garage. It's mostly empty, except for a tool bench on one side and a few stacked boxes against another.

Kyler happily ambles over to them and peels back the top flap on one. "Hey! Decorations for days. There's even one of those elf on the shelf things, although it looks like an ancient elf. No way, there's a set of hockey skates and skiing ornaments. Dude—this was meant to be." He cackles and holds them out for me to see.

Still trying to feel my feet, I whirl a finger in the air. "No snowmobile."

He holds up some pretty silver tinsel. "This is nice. Come on, you like it, right? It would look awesome on a tree with those hockey skates."

I don't respond. As I'm wiggling my toes to get the feeling back in them, he moves a box. I notice him clenching and unclenching his fist. I get the feeling that when he was talking to the neighbors, he wasn't telling the truth about that injury.

"Your hand's bothering you," I say gently.

He drops it to his side. "It's fine."

"Is that what the doctors said?"

The smirk's gone as he picks through a box. "The doctors say I need surgery, but if I do that..." He stops and takes a breath. "Look, you can't tell your brother. I haven't told anyone yet, and he keeps asking when I'll be back."

"Ah..."

"They told me I need the surgery now, and if I get it, I'm out for the whole season."

My mouth opens. I might not like hockey, but I love my brother, and I know how hard the past month has been for him. He's been stepping up, but because it was a temporary situation. The other right winger is nowhere near as talented as Kyler, and I'm not sure Will can hold the Predators in first place unless he has the Beast in his lineup. "Are you sure?"

He presses his lips together. "I've gotten more than one opinion. It's all the same. But I don't know." He looks down at his hand. "I think maybe I could—"

"And make it worse?" I stare at him. I know hockey injuries. My brother has had plenty. "You should get it fixed. There'll be other seasons."

That's not the answer he's looking for. "You sound like *them*. This is our best season. We're in first. Everything's aligning. If I come back, we have a chance at winning it all."

"Not *everything's* aligning. If it gets worse—"

"Enough," he snaps, his back tense as he bends over the

box he's looking through. He immediately regrets it; his shoulders slump, and the next time he speaks, his voice is softer. "Sorry for being harsh. I know what my options are. I was going to make the decision after Cabo."

Every bit of the tension on his face, I *feel*. I saw it when he was talking to the neighbors. You can give your best, clawing to finally pop your head above water, only to get knocked down by another wave. Will's a legend. It must be awfully hard, standing in the shadow of someone like that and wanting only to be at your best to support them.

I know. I've done it all my life.

Maybe he does know a little more about me than I give him credit for.

I peek into the box and grin. "Oh my gosh. I haven't seen this game in forever! Milles Borne!"

He stares at it, confused, as I tuck it under my arm.

"Come on, I'll teach you how to play."

"We're going to play a game?"

I nod, getting a tingle of excitement. "Yep."

As I head for the door, he starts to follow.

I turn back. "Bring the decoration box, too. Maybe a little decorating wouldn't hurt."

Chapter 12
Kyler

"*Coup Fourré!*" Iris shouts in triumph, laying down her driving-wheel card and saying, "Give me an accident? I don't *think* so!"

I have no idea what happened. She's been explaining the rules and we've played a dozen hands, but I still don't know what's going on. It has something to do with a car race, but there are so many cards and actions to take I can't keep track.

Throwing my cards down, I say, "Does that mean you win?" I tip back in my chair and look out the window: still snowing.

I should be happy, because for once in her life, Iris isn't looking like it's the end of the world.

"No, but I'm winning," she says greedily, putting down a 200. "Your turn."

I pick up the cards, not sure what my next move should be. Right now, I can't stop thinking of Camryn and Cady, the twelve-year-old twins. I should've mailed them something a week ago. They're at that age where they really care about gifts, and the only time they actually acknowledge me is when they thank me for my Christmas gifts. They're not jerks—they're the cutest kids—but I'm not exactly present in their day-to-day lives, so it's gotten increasingly awkward whenever we do talk.

I don't have much family, so the family I do have, I want to hold on to really tight. But my sister Deena is married to a hotshot plastic surgeon in California, and he has about ten siblings, plus they all have kids, too. It's a big family...and they don't need one more. I'm never going to be the cool uncle. More like the *forgotten* uncle.

Doesn't matter that I'm in the NHL. The first time I met Dr. Plastic, he said, "In this family, we're bigger baseball fans." So, anything I can do to stay in their memory, I do it.

Putting down a card on the playing surface, I wonder how much longer we have to do this.

"You can't play that card," Iris warns.

"My bad." I pick it up again and stare at my options. I have no clue.

She stacks her cards and says, "How about we break for lunch?"

"Yeah. Good."

She's watching me as I help her clean up. "Wanna try the chicken and hash browns?"

I nod, not really thinking about food, which is odd for me. I'm thinking about how much further I have to fall until no one thinks about me at all.

She nudges my shoulder. "After this, we can decorate. Do you think we can get a tree?"

I get the feeling she's only saying that because she sees I've devolved into a grumpy mood. "We don't have to."

"What are you talking about? I want to. I think it'll cheer us up," she says, smiling as she goes to the kitchen. She glances at me. "Are you sure you're okay?"

"Yeah. Just thinking of my nieces. I forgot to get them stuff before I came, and now it's too late. I mean, I could trek to the convenience store and buy something with the mountains on it, like a keychain, but I have nowhere to ship it. The mail isn't running, or we would have seen it pass by."

She tilts her head. "What are they into?"

I shrug. "I have no idea. All I know is that it's going to be really late getting to them."

Her eyes light up. "Do they have their ears pierced?"

I nod, recalling sending them each a pair of small diamond earrings for their birthday a few years ago.

She disappears and returns a second later holding up a pair of earrings for my inspection. They look like strawberries, made of red yarn. Yep, the twins would probably love those. They'd probably *fight* over those.

"Okay...only problem is, I have two nieces."

She laughs. "I'm not saying these. These are mine. I crocheted them. I can teach you to crochet. Lemons, pineapples, cherries, apples—whatever you want."

I look down at my hand. I'm not really sure I could even make some silly earrings, the way my hand is. That's how far I've fallen. "I don't..."

"It's easy. You can do it one-handed." She grins. "Would they like them?"

"Yeah. I think so."

"And you can even stitch their initials in them. What fruit?"

"Let's just focus on the fruit. Can you do a banana?"

"Can *I* do a banana? No. *You* are going to do this," she says, patting my back.

Apparently, Iris is a crafter, and a pretty good one. She pulls out a drawer from her suitcase that has an entire stash of supplies. Sitting next to me at the table, she removes skeins of yarn, needles, hoops, and hooks. She goes through the process slowly as she shows me how to make the loops for a banana. Chewing on my bottom lip like I do when I play hockey, I spend the next hour learning how to make the earrings. I'm terrible at first and have to restart three different times, but she doesn't say anything. Finally, I get the motions with one hand, and I'm so engrossed in the rhythm that I don't notice when she gets up and goes to the kitchen to make our lunch.

It's comforting to hear the clank of silverware and plates. I glance up and offer to help, but she tells me to sit and keep crocheting. I try, but before long I'm watching her as she glides around, putting the trays in the oven then opening the fridge to make a garden salad. She chops tomatoes and cucumbers and sprinkles them into a bowl of lettuce. She hums a little, and I smirk at how off key she is.

The warmth of the cabin and the buttery smell of the food cooking makes me feel, well, at home. I set aside my earrings and get us both waters to drink.

As I take a bite of the juicy chicken, I can't help but notice the way her green eyes light up when she talks about her favorite art gallery in Nashville. I tell her about the coffee shop I like to go to in Brentwood that makes cider donuts in the fall, and she tells me she'll try it out.

The conversation flows easily between us, and I find myself laughing more than I have in a while. She tells me about her job as a boot designer and how she loves the creative, chaotic nature of it. We talk about books and movies and realize we both hate horror but love biographies.

After lunch, I offer to do the dishes, but she says she likes doing it because it gives her time to think. After that, she curls up in the chair next to the window with Puck in her lap as she reads through a book she brought. She's engrossed in the story by the time I have two pairs of banana earrings that look decent.

"Not bad," I say as I examine my work. True, they're not perfect, but I'm thinking of writing a little note to go with them and explaining about my experience of being stuck on a mountain with someone who taught me how to crochet. They'll get a kick out of it, especially if I go into detail about how I rescued someone and her rat from a bear outside the cabin.

"All done?" Iris asks as she sets her book down. A slow smile curves her face, and I inhale a sharp breath at how genuine and sweet it is.

I clear my throat as she starts to put her supplies back in the drawer.

"Where'd you learn to make all this stuff?"

She shrugs. "Well...Will is good at everything, in case you didn't notice. Believe it or not, I was the first one in the family on skates. Every time I would find something I liked, he would come in and outshine me. So, I started designing and making my own clothes and jewelry because I knew it was something he'd never want to do. You've seen him—he wears the same outfit until it can practically walk by itself."

I chuckle. That's one way—of many—he and I are alike, and it's just like I thought; no wonder she hates hockey. My parents spent a hell of a lot of time and money to get me where I am today. It has a way of swallowing up a family's quality time, and it's probably overshadowed most of her life.

"Thanks," I tell her, pointing to the jewelry. "For these. I never knew I had the talent."

She laughs, her cheeks reddening. "I enjoyed watching you."

"I thought you were reading your book."

She lowers her lashes. "I was peeking at your progress most of the time."

"Why? You didn't think I could do it?"

"I imagine you can do just about anything you want."

"Oh."

We wind up staring at each other for a beat too long, until it becomes uncomfortable. In that moment, I begin to wonder what her lips taste like.

Quickly, I look away. I'm not making the mistake of coming on to my teammate's little sister, but damn if her lips don't look so sweet...

Dragging my hands down my face, I take a deep breath. It's cabin fever, driving me insane. That's all.

"I'm going to go out and look for a tree," I announce.

She looks up from giving Puck a pet. "Are you sure? Do you think you can get one? Do you need an axe?"

I throw on a jacket. "I saw one in the garage."

"Want me to come with you?"

My first thought—yeah, I do. Which is crazy because it's her, and even crazier since I shouldn't want her anywhere near me.

I shake my head. "Stay. You don't have the footwear. I'll be back in an hour."

"Okay..." She looks hurt.

All my instincts are begging me to go over there and fold her up in my arms. I turn and march away before I can give in to them.

When I'm outside in the swirling snow, I take a deep breath, allowing me to come to my senses. The air is frigid and gray, and the snow shows no sign of stopping. I wade through thigh-deep powder, grab the axe, throw it over my shoulder, and head out. Down the driveway, I find my car, right where I left it, covered in drifts. From here, I can see the smoke coming from the Davis' chimney and not much else. I wonder if they're using their binoculars to watch me.

Brushing the snow off the front of the car, I notice a small dent in the bumper where it hit the ditch and remind myself it was Iris's fault. That doesn't help. She was freaking adorable, helping me make those crafts, patient. And her edamame might be the devil's junk food, but she made a mean salad, not to mention she's pretty damn funny when she's trying to beat me at cards.

I can't be getting interested in Iris. She loathes me and everything I stand for.

Hearing a frantic yipping, I turn to find Puck bounding through my footprints. He looks a little like a drunken sailor, so deliriously happy he doesn't care if he's about to get himself killed.

"What are you doing, rat?" I say, realizing what this means.

A second later, I see a pink blur coming my way. As I blink the snowflakes from my eyes, the image of Iris comes into focus. She's changed into a fuzzy pink sweater with white ski pants. She steps gingerly through the snow toward me. "Fine one yet?"

I push the axe up on my shoulder, hoping I appear manly. "What are you doing here?"

"I thought you might need help."

Yeah...not sure what kind of help she can give me. "I'm good. You go wait inside where it's warm."

"I'm fine," she says, and she's smiling so sweetly I don't want her to, either.

"All right." I point to a small pine a few feet away. "That one?"

She tilts her head. "Too bare."

Another. "Too small."

I whirl and point at yet another.

She wrinkles her nose and shakes her head, then her eyes light up at something in the distance. "That one!"

It's far off, and it's probably bigger than the house. "That thing's huge."

"No, it's not." She starts to carefully push through the snow, making her way there.

"Trees out in nature look smaller than they actually are," I mutter, not that that slows her roll. She actually speeds up if you can call that awkward lumber she's doing speedy.

"This is it! Definitely," she proclaims as soon as she's standing beside it.

She doesn't seem to notice that it's almost three times taller than she is. Okay, she's a runt, but I'm not looking forward to dragging that thing back to the house. "It's huge."

"It's *perfect*."

"I think I saw a Christmas movie about this very thing," I say, tilting my head to imagine it in the living room of the cabin. "It didn't end well."

"It's an A-frame. Can't we just plop it in the middle of the house?"

I roll my eyes. "No."

"Whatever. Do you need help chopping it down?" she asks, looking at my hand.

I let out a breath, and it clouds in front of me. I shouldn't have said anything about my injury. "Like you know how to swing an axe?"

"How hard can it be?"

I hold it by the shoulder and offer the handle up to her.

She takes it, a little surprised, and then her brow wrinkles in determination. "No problem. Stand back."

I do as she says as she grasps the axe firmly, preparing to swing it. "Impressive grip," I tell her with a smirk.

"I actually learned that from Jack in *Titanic*, that movie you found in the attic," she says over her shoulder, getting into chopping position. Then, letting out a loud grunt I didn't know she was capable of, she lets the blade fly.

It doesn't even chip the bark.

"What the—" She looks at the bit. "The damn thing is too dull."

I take it from her. "Watch the master work."

The trunk isn't small. It takes at least twenty good hacks. After the first strike, I can't feel the fingers of my right hand anymore, but she's watching carefully, excitedly cheering me on when she sees progress, so I keep going. It's my flaw—I hate letting anyone down.

By the time the tree falls, the tingles are traveling up my elbow.

"Timber!" she shouts excitedly as I massage my arm. I stop when she turns to me, flushed and excited, but not fast enough. Her face falls. "Kyler...oh no, I'm so sorry. Did you hurt it?"

I shake my head. "It's good."

She rushes to me, taking my hand gently in both of hers. "What does it feel like?"

I want to feel her gloved fingers on mine, but I don't.

"Nothing," I say, snatching my hand back. "It feels like nothing."

Chapter 13

Iris

One thing is pretty obvious as we set to decorating: Ed and Riana, the owners, are Christmas crazy.

The boxes we found in the garage are only the tip of the iceberg. We found more in the attic space above, and they're packed with items, enough to make the cozy cabin into a wintertime wonderland. Someone in the house clearly had a love of snowmen because I keep pulling them out of the boxes—snowmen skiing, snowmen baking bread, snowmen in hats and coats, snowmen singing carols, a snowman peeking sheepishly out of an outhouse. I set up each and every one as Kyler wrangles the tree into the metal stand we found.

When he has it set up, I clap my hands. "I told you it was perfect!"

It actually nearly scrapes the ceiling of the living area, which has to be at least thirteen feet tall. We had trouble dragging it back and through the doors, but now that it's here, it looks like it belongs.

I nudge him. "Who was right? Come on, say it."

His lips twist. He was upset about his hand when we first came in, but now I think he's starting to have fun. "I still think it's damn big."

"Big, but *amazing*! I knew it would look perfect in this room. The loft in my mom's house was my bedroom growing up. It has high ceilings, too, and I always wanted a tree like this in it."

He gives me an amused look. "Are you always this happy when you decorate?"

Yes. Yes, I am. I clap my hands and run to get the white twinkle lights I found. "It's going to be gorgeous!"

Okay, he does have a point...I underestimated the struggle of wrapping the lights around a tree this big. By the time I get done adding them and the tinsel, I'm out of breath and sweaty from climbing up and down the ladder.

But he's right; I'm happy. It's weird, because that feeling—that warm, gushy feeling I only get when celebrating Christmas with my family? I sort of feel it now, too, and I have to wonder if it's not just the Christmas spirit. It might be the company, too.

It's odd because I feel as if I've known Kyler for longer than just two days. I glance over at him. He's the kind of man you'd want around in case of the zombie apocalypse or any end-of-the-world event. Sure, he's prone to running around naked, but he knows how to make fire and chop down trees.

"Now for the star!"

He holds up his hands. "You're on your own."

I give him a playful poke in the ribs. "Give me a boost."

He eyes the top of the tree, then me. "You're kidding, right?"

"No. I was a cheerleader, for a...season. Half a season. Whatever. Just lift me up to stand on your shoulders, hold on to my ankles, and I'll throw that sucker on."

He eyes me cautiously then stoops to the ground, motioning for me to climb up. Straddling his back, I prop myself on his shoulders, holding on to his head with one hand, balancing the star in the other as he rises to standing. Then, he helps me lift one foot onto his shoulder. It's actually scarier than I thought it would be. The ground looks so far away, and I'm clutching his head so tight I might leave a mark.

"Ow, loosen up," he growls as I'm trying to bring my second foot to his shoulder.

I do, only when I've got my balance. Rising up shakily, I feel his hands, sure and steady, on my calves. This is perfect, the top branch of the tree in reaching distance. Slowly and carefully, I lean forward and place the star.

"I think I got—" At that moment, I make the mistake of looking down and topple forward, then back, then lose my balance completely, and down I go.

Only to fall right into his arms. He's so close I can feel his heart beating against mine. His breath fans my face, and as we lock eyes, time seems to slip away.

He murmurs, "*You* were a cheerleader?"

That snaps me out of whatever moment we're having. I slip out of his arms, blushing. "Just one thing of many I tried—and failed—in order to compete with my brother."

We stand back and look at the tree in all its glory. With all the twinkling lights, it's a sight.

But something's off.

He's the first to say, "It's tilting."

Yes, it most definitely is, but I'm not going back up there again, and not just because of the scary heights. What happened after I fell was almost as frightening. Being warm and cozy against his chest felt so right. It was delicious and perfect, and ugh, I have to stop.

I let out a grunt. "Screw it. If we drink enough, it'll be perfectly straight. Where's the wine?"

"I like the way you think."

He smiles at me, and I smile back then his eyes drop to my lips. For a moment, I think he might try to kiss me.

Oh my god. Kyler Blanchette wants to kiss me.

What's scarier is that I want him to.

Quickly, I turn away and run to the bedroom then come back out with a box. "I have a surprise for you."

He eyes it with doubt. "I hope it's not more ornaments because honestly, we've put them everywhere in the cabin."

I giggle. It's true. We even set out knickknacks in the kitchen. He draped tinsel and pine boughs around the bay window, and I decorated the countertops with snowmen. But no, this is different. I found it at the top of the closet in the bedroom.

"Open it," I say, grinning from ear to ear.

He narrows his eyes. "Is Puck inside and planning to jump out at me?"

"He's by the fire."

He glances over. "Ah, yes, enjoying the fruits of my

labor. Fine, give me the box." Clearing his throat, he cautiously opens it and pulls out a Norwegian-style red Christmas sweater. It's a bit faded and there's a hole on one of the elbows, but I'm almost positive it will fit his broad shoulders.

He gazes at it, a smile growing. "You found me a Christmas sweater."

I nod excitedly. "And the best part is, I have a red turtleneck and this adorable pink skirt with hearts on it and red cowboy boots! We can be twins for the holidays."

"For today, I guess. Hopefully we'll be gone before Sunday gets here."

Some of my thrill at imagining us in matching outfits fades. I shrug. "I just thought it might save you from wearing the same thing every day."

"Let me try it on." He unbuttons his shirt, slowly. My heart pounds as he shrugs out of it and I get to see him—once again—in his male perfection, from his golden skin to his delectable eight-pack. My breath hitches. The physique on him is droolworthy.

I poke him in the chest. "What are you waiting for, a photo shoot? Put the sweater on, Kyler. Geeze."

"Iris," he sings. "You like my body."

"Pfft. I've seen enough of your chest and junk in my time, thank you very much. You aren't special."

"I am, princess. But I won't embarrass you." He slides on the sweater, and yes, it's tight, but it looks amazing. His mahogany hair is a little ruffled, and I reach out and tame the curls away from his face.

He starts for a moment then grabs my hand and pulls me to him until we're inches apart. I study the golden stria-

Christmas Cupid

tions in his brown eyes, the scars on his face, the divot in his nose. Taken separately, they're nothing special, but put them together and oh boy I'm in trouble.

It's as if he's daring me to make a move, giving me an opportunity to decide if I want to be this close to him. Then Liam's face flashes in my head, and I pull away, keeping a smile on my face.

I say lightly, "This is kinda weird. Different."

He clears his throat. "What do you mean?"

"I just never thought I'd be here, enjoying myself, with *you*, an actual hockey player. You know how when you're in a crisis situation with someone and one day together can really equal ten days? Like you go through so much in a short period of time, so you feel like you've actually spent more time with them? Sort of like the people on *The Walking Dead*. I mean, I don't like scary stuff, but I did watch the show because of Daryl Dixon—he's the perfect person you'd want with you if things went south. I've got you in that category. We haven't spent much time together, yet it feels like more because we've been scrambling around trying to survive this cabin together. You're not that slobbering idiot who came on to me last New Year's Eve."

He nods and looks down at his hand. "A lot has happened since then."

I was messing with the tree but turn to him. "Oh. So, what are you saying? The Beast is off his game? When you're the Beast, you're hitting on everything that moves. Now, you're actually...human."

He's quiet. "You're right. I'm no one unless I'm scoring goals on the ice."

I frown. That wasn't what I meant. "You think that's all you are?"

He doesn't answer, but I can fill in the blanks. Yes.

"You know what I think? I think you're afraid to let go of it because you're worried that's the best thing you'll ever be. But you know..." I shrug. "It might be the best to some people, but not everyone. Other people use a different gauge to measure a person."

Again, he's quiet. I can tell he doesn't believe me.

If he only sees that gauge, if he thinks a person's worth is based on how talented they are on the playing field then I guess I don't have to worry about him wanting me for more than just a quick hook-up. I'm not sporty. Sure, I excel at artsy stuff, but I'm thinking that doesn't rate with him.

How disappointing.

"Besides, it's not forever. You really think it would be so terrible waiting six months to play again?"

He shakes his head. "It's not just that. People are depending on me."

Oh, right. I'm sure this stems from ol' Captain Slappy's pep talk prior to the game that talks about how every part of the Predator machine is essential. It's nice and inspirational, but it's also a load of bunk. He'll tell you there's no I in team, but he wants to be the capital T.

"Like my brother?" I snort. "Believe me, he will be fine. He's a great guy, but you should know by now he doesn't share the spotlight well. In fact, he *likes* doing everything himself. He lives for it. I can understand you being sore because they might win the Cup this year without you... but I wouldn't worry about letting Slappy down."

He looks down at his hand, doubtful.

"As much as my brother loves playing with you—and you know he does—I know he loves *you* more, the healthy, one hundred percent you. He'd want you to get better."

I grab his hand, holding it in both my hands. It's huge, almost the size of both of mine combined. I know what a hockey player's hands mean. Yes, they're usually in gloves, but if a player's hands aren't working right, they don't have the proper stick control, and that's essential.

Gently, I run a finger over the knuckle, waiting for him to say something, but he doesn't. "You don't believe me," I finally say, to fill the silence.

He shakes his head. "No, I'm just thinking of you...as a *cheerleader*."

Dropping his hand, I smack him on the shoulder, but as hard as his body is, it probably hurts me more. "Ass. I'm going to put on my Christmassy clothes and make dinner."

"It's not Christmas yet."

I sniff. "Stop being a Grinch. I'm in the spirit, and once it hits, oh boy, just you wait. You may be the Beast on ice, but I'm the Beast of Christmas."

He runs his palms down his sweater as if to smooth it, puts his hands on his hips, and gives me a smirk. "Bring it on, sweetheart."

Chapter 14

Kyler

I almost kissed her.

Though every fiber of my being is telling me otherwise, it would've been a bad thing. My life is already complicated. I can't complicate it more by hooking up with my best friend's sister. Though after what he pulled, maybe he deserves it. Unless...

Unless this wasn't a practical joke.

As Iris moves around the kitchen, opening cabinets and drawers, I look down at Puck. Will got her that dog to cheer her up. They've always been close. He's always been ultra-protective of her, willing to do anything to make her happy...

Hell, maybe he didn't do this as a practical joke. Maybe he wanted this to happen.

Bing Crosby is crooning in the background, smooth, sweet tunes, and yet Iris looks like she's in the mood for thrashing heavy metal. Why is she pissy? Why can't I understand her?

I move into the kitchen and lean against the center island. She has that *Stay away* scowl on her face like she wants to murder someone, and knives are within grabbing distance, so I won't offer to help. "Whatcha making?"

With her hair framing her face and her red lips and flirty skirt and cowboy boots, she looks like a snack I want to eat. But I can't say that.

She starts to whisk something. "Salmon. I don't care if you don't like it. You can eat snow for all I care."

"Look, I didn't mean that, about the cheerleader stuff. I'm sure you made a very good one," I say, kicking myself for having made the comment in the first place. It was mostly to get the image of her in my arms when I caught her out of my head. "And I'm glad we're matching."

Never breaking her rhythm with the bowl, she says, "I was actually a terrible cheerleader. I broke two guys' noses with my roundoff, and they invited me not to come back."

I stare at her. "That's...terrible." Terrible, but also... hilarious. "Invited you...?"

She stops whisking. Her pissed-off mug disintegrates, and slowly, she begins to laugh.

I join in.

She sighs. "I've always been a terrible klutz. That's why I don't do any sports. You know how much it sucks being terrible at everything in a family with Will Miller?"

"Hey, that's bull. You make all those crafty things, and you do a mean scrambled egg. And...whatever this is." I point.

She looks into the bowl. "Poached salmon with orange glaze."

"Mm. Sounds amazing."

A smile breaks out on her lips. "Well…thanks."

"You're not that terrible after all, Iris."

She starts. "What do you mean?"

"I mean, it took me a full day to get over that right hook you gave me last year."

She looks down, sheepish. "It was just a slap, and I had a very good reason for that."

I cross my arms. "I'd like to hear it."

"You dated an acquaintance of mine, Mara, didn't you? She said you were a dog."

I frown.

"You don't remember?"

I shrug. "I don't remember having *dated* anyone. Who has time for that? I've got a career. I'm on the road half the time and in practice the rest of it."

"Eh, that's exactly what Will says, and yet you have plenty of time for parties."

"All this judging." I make a tsk sound with my tongue. "You never have the urge to pull that stick out of your ass and enjoy life?"

She presses her lips together. "I like parties. Civilized ones."

"And ours wasn't?"

"It was a kegger."

"Okay, maybe we had a keg. So what? I'm a civilized person."

"But Mara said you stood her up for dinner after you two hooked up then you never returned her texts. That's dog behavior." At her feet, Puck whines. "Sorry, Rob. That's *worse* than dog behavior."

I laugh. "I don't even remember said date. I don't

remember any girl called Mara that I hooked up with. I guess we might have gotten our wires crossed. Maybe she meant another hockey player. Where did she meet me?"

"At the Wild Horse Saloon downtown."

I smirk. "I've never been—I swear. I don't do country music, and I honestly don't care for bars. There're too many people around. I like to hang out at my friends' houses. That's where I meet people."

She cocks her head. "Mara did say she'd had too much to drink, but she was sure it was you."

"I never give my number out randomly. If I had set up a date after a hook-up, I would have gone. I'm not an asshole."

She sighs. "Okay, maybe it wasn't you she met."

"Ah, but did you really have to take it out on my jaw? Seems excessive."

She gives me a sheepish look. "I'll admit I wasn't in the best of moods to begin with. The guy I had been dating for years—the one I thought was my happily-ever-after—had just left me for his research assistant. Will invited me to that party thinking he could cheer me up, but the last thing I needed was a drunken hook-up with another player like my brother. And yet that was all that was available. I was really sad, and...I took it out on you." She shrugs. "Sorry."

"Wow."

She eyes me. "Wow, what?"

"I'm still trying to comprehend the first part—that any guy would do that to a girl he's invested years of his life with. Someone like you."

Her eyes narrow. She thinks it's an insult.

"I mean, if anyone deserves that happily-ever-after thing...it's you."

She stares. "What do you..."

I point to the stuff she's making. "I mean, you're a great cook. You design boots, you knit, you clean—"

"Wait." She looks disgusted. "Is this some sort of sexist—"

"No." This is coming out all wrong. I don't know why I want to impress her, but I do. Usually, it's not this hard to talk to a girl. I take a breath and try again. "What I mean is, you're wickedly talented, maybe not in sports but in other things, funny, sweet, cute—no, gorgeous...I mean, you're the total package. Who would want to leave you?"

A cute blush fires on her cheeks.

"And you're right, about hockey. I mean, we do look like idiots, getting all excited about it. It's just a game. There is a whole world beyond sports. It shouldn't be that big a deal to me."

She spins to the sink, running the water, then turns back to me, pouring some vegetables onto a tray. "I get why it is. If I ever found a sport I was good at and trained as much as my brother did, I'd probably hate to give it up, too. Even for a few months."

"Yeah. But you know, maybe I'll find my calling in... making food." I reach over to pick up the whisk.

"I wouldn't count on it," she says on a laugh as she grabs the whisk from me, and I go to goose her.

As I reach for her, I realize I could just as easily pull her to me and kiss her. Somehow, I resist, and she shrieks and lurches forward, sending orange-colored liquid flying through the air. A cold slap of it slashes across my face.

Christmas Cupid

I stick my tongue out and take a lick. Yum. Then I reach for the bowl and a spoon, pointing it at her. "You're dead."

She makes an O with her mouth and runs off as I dash around the island and come to face her. There's nowhere to hide. I hold the spoon up, dripping with orange sauce.

"Don't," she warns. "That's supposed to go on the salmon."

"Are you sure? Because it looks really good on me, and I think it'll look better on you."

I advance, and she backs up against the pantry door, shrieking some more. "No! I'm sorry, I'm sorry, I'm sorry!" she shouts again, doubling over and laughing.

I'm chuckling as I grab her in my arms and hold the spoon over her, dotting her face with it. "Looks amazing. And I bet it's better than that crusty crap you put on last night."

She wriggles free, gazing at me with a defiant vengeance. "That crusty crap is $200 an ounce." She wipes the gunk off her cheek and holds it in her palm, ready to smear on me. "And I'm going to kill you."

I smirk. "I don't think I should be worried, knowing your athletic abilities."

Of course, she picks this time to hit the bullseye. When she tosses the sauce, she hits me right in the nose. I reach for a handful in the bowl, but she says, "Wait, wait, wait. Really, stop. I have to make food with this."

I do as she says, warily presenting the bowl to her in case she gets any other ideas, but she doesn't.

Still grinning, she takes the salmon out and begins to glaze it. "I hope I have enough."

Standing next to her, I notice she still has some of it on her cheek. I run a finger along it, gently scooping it up, and taste it: just like the other taste I had, but better. Because of her.

She turns and looks up at me, her pouty lips begging to be kissed. Then her serious expression gives way, and she giggles. Probably because I have orange sauce dripping off my chin.

"Let me get that," she says, using a finger to flick the drop away. She tastes it. "Mmm."

Then she licks her lips. She's still begging for it, and I can't resist. I've got to do this. Now. There'll never be a better time.

I lower my mouth to hers, pausing a hair's breadth away to make sure she wants this too.

She doesn't move away. This is going to happen.

As I'm about to move in, there's a knock on the door. We spring apart, and I find myself being dragged farther away from the thing I want. I want to go back, but the moment is broken and she's looking toward the door now.

"Who could that be?"

I shake my head. Whoever they are, I'm going to tear them a new one because they have the worst timing ever.

I notice it's dark outside as I move to the door. When did that happen? For the past few hours, I haven't cared about a damn thing outside. Everything I've wanted has been in here.

Then I notice Joan Davis's smiling face. I open the door, and she says, "Hey, neighbor! Glad you're still kicking!"

As nice as she is, I *want* to do some kicking. Like her, out of here. "Yeah..."

She notices my face and points to her cheek. "You've got some..."

"Oh." I swipe at it, and it just serves to make me more restless. I should be kissing Iris right now, tasting her skin, not this. "Why are you here?"

"Just noticed you hadn't been digging out and wanted to make sure you had everything you needed," she says as I notice the blue lights behind her cutting through the darkness. I also notice that the snow has let up. There are only a few flakes drifting through the air. "Anyway, Hal, one of the forest rangers, came to check on us, and I told him you could use some help getting your car out of the pickle it's in. He pulled it out so you can drive it when the roads up here get cleared." She smiles.

I look over her shoulder to see Hal, an older wiry man in a big bulky coat and a cowboy-style hat. Several feet away, he stands next to a brown truck and sends me a wave.

I wave back, feeling odd. I didn't even hear them pulling my car out of the ditch.

Because you were having fun with Iris, my brain says.

"Oh...yeah...I..."

Iris comes rushing up behind me. "The snow's stopped?"

Joan laughs. "Stopped hours ago! What have you two been doing?"

"Decorating," Iris says lamely, looking at me. "We thought..."

"I knew you two wanted to get off this mountain, you know, since you don't know each other. Hal said he's happy to drive you into town if you're in a hurry. Roads are clearing up good there. They didn't get nearly as much snow as we did."

Iris gets a glazed look on her face. "Oh...it's really late."

I look at her. "Yeah...I mean, not tonight. I'm going to head out bright and early tomorrow morning. Don't you think?"

We just stare at each other for the longest time, until Joan shifts in the doorway and Hal calls out, "Who's coming with me? Young lady?"

Iris sucks in a breath as if she's thinking then sends him a wave. "Actually, we've already cooked dinner, so I think I'm going to stay here tonight. But thank you for checking on us."

I smile in triumph.

Hal tips his hat at us. "Stay as long as you like. The snowplows will be here tomorrow."

I nod and wave goodbye then shut the door. I turn to Iris. Her big green eyes blink at me.

"So...dinner?" she asks.

"Dinner," I say. "But first..."

I close the distance between us. Her eyes are locked on mine, her lips parted and awaiting me. I can't resist a second longer; I have to have her.

I slip my hand around her neck, threading my fingers through the thick waves of her hair. She breathes out a whisper of pleasure that sends shivers down my spine. My mouth moves toward hers, and when our lips meet, there's an electric spark that arches between us.

This time, there's no slap. She sighs against me and

opens her mouth slightly, letting me slip my tongue in. She gasps as I deepen the kiss, my hands firmly cupping her face as if to stop time for just one moment longer. Her citrusy scent fills each breath I take between kisses, and the brush of her sweater against me is like liquid fire. Her body melts into mine as she clutches my shirt, her breasts pressing urgently against me.

The map might say we're on a mountain in Tennessee, but for the first time in my life, I could swear I'm in heaven.

We both need this. The tension that's been hovering over us, the long, secretive glances we've been sending each other today...I've never wanted anything more than this delicious heat. I want to devour her. I want to take her hard and fast. I want to bury myself in her.

I push her back against the wall and bring my mouth down to her neck, and she murmurs in pleasure as I suck softly along the pulse. She writhes against me, her delicate hands slipping under my sweater to clutch at my back, her fingers digging into my skin.

A surge of lust washes over me. I can't keep my hands off her, touching her cheek, her hair, the bend of her shoulder, her fluttering lashes, and soon I'm tugging at her sweater. She gasps again as I suck on her tongue, and it should be wrong, the way I'm kissing my best friend's sister, but it feels so right.

She helps me take off her shirt, her throat moving rapidly as I toss it behind me. The soft light of the hallway catches on her exposed breasts in a red lacy bra. She stares at me for a second, eyes wide and cheeks flushed. She closes her eyes.

"Keep them open, Iris." My voice is hoarse as if it's been dragged over gravel.

Her green gaze holds mine, and for a moment I'm at a loss as to what I should do.

Just go with your instincts.

I want her. I bring my hands up to cup the soft swell of her breasts, enjoying the weight of them in my hands. She lets out a soft moan, pushing them into my palms as flames lick inside of me.

I lean down and kiss the curve of her chest, and then I give a little peck to the part of her nipple that pokes over the edge of her bra. She moans again.

Then I give a quick kiss to the other one, and finally I give it a little lick. She moves her hips against mine. This time I suck hard as I flick my tongue against the pebbled peaks, and I hear her rapidly breathing as she says my name. I pick her up, and her legs wrap around my waist as I go back to her lips and devour her lushness.

"Jesus. Iris," I groan—just as a burning smell wafts into the hallway. *Ignore it*, the lizard side of my brain says while the other side worries about a fire. Breathing heavily, I dip my face into her neck, trying to catch my breath. "Something is on fire somewhere. Do you care?"

She drops her legs and blinks up at me with a dazed look. "Oven. Asparagus. Must save."

She gives me a little push and maneuvers around me to pick up her sweater.

"Iris?" I ask, my tone incredulous.

Without looking at me, she adjusts her shirt then clears her throat. "That was, um, interesting, but not a great idea. I'll check on them."

Interesting? Like us kissing is a science experiment? I frown. That hurts. It really does. It probably shouldn't, but there it is.

She flounces down the hall and into the kitchen. I hear the clanging of pots, and I rub my hands down my face then press my fingers to my temple. Now I'll have to face her at dinner.

Chapter 15

Iris

I stand in the kitchen, my heart racing from Kyler and his kisses. He's everything I've sworn to avoid: my brother's best friend, a hockey player, and definitely not my type. Yet there's something about him that makes me feel like I'm having fun for the first time in ages. Our banter, his unexpected vulnerability—heck, I even like it when he calls me a brat...

It's so confusing.

I focus on finishing dinner, the salmon sizzling in the pan, its aroma mingling with the scent of the orange sauce and herbs. I set the table, the clink of cutlery and the rustle of napkins a welcome distraction in the cozy, golden-lit kitchen of the cabin.

But despite the comforting surroundings, I feel fragile, a whirlwind of emotions I don't know how to navigate. What am I doing? What do I want?

I hear the front door opening and I walk to the foyer,

only to catch a glimpse of Kyler, coat on, flashlight in hand as he steps outside.

"Kyler?" I ask, but he's already slammed the door.

I press my hands against the cool glass as I watch him, my eyes intent on his every move. He strides across the snow with a purposeful gait, and the wind ruffles his hair like fingers combing through locks of silk. His posture speaks volumes of troubles that swirl in his mind.

He stops in front of a large tree, head tilted back to take in the exquisite night sky, a deep black abyss illuminated with twinkling stars.

My heart thrums with anticipation as I long to get close to him, to feel his strength and warmth wrap around me like a blanket. A tingle runs down my spine at the memory of being held in his strong arms, a feeling I haven't experienced in what seems like an eternity. But fear grips me tight, fear of rejection and fear of taking a chance on someone again keeping me rooted to my spot by the window.

A profound sadness washes over me, and it takes all my control not to go out there, to ask him what's wrong and why he looks so lost. Something holds me back from taking that leap of faith.

I turn to Rob, who's also watching him. He whines. *Come on, Mom, go out there and talk to him. Mr. Grizzly might come back.*

"I think he wants to be alone. Sometimes people need to just be alone with their thoughts. It's how they move on."

Like how you're alone in this cabin and the seriously amazing guy is outside?

"Are you playing matchmaker with me and Mr. Hockey Player out there?"

He barks.

"Ugh. You know it was a bad idea to kiss him." I sigh as my eyes find Kyler near his car, looking out into the distance. "I wonder if the snow reminds him of Vermont, and I wonder if that makes him extra sad on the holidays."

You were sad until you met him. Rob tilts his head, his big eyes seeming to understand my turmoil, or maybe he's just hoping for a treat. After giving him a cookie, I wait another fifteen minutes for Kyler to come back inside for dinner, then I sit down to eat, the food tasting bland despite the rich flavors.

"I wish he were here even if we argued," I tell Rob as I slip him a piece of tomato from the salad I made earlier, and he chomps on it. "You know, this is Cupid's Cabin. Maybe there's something about it that makes you feel drawn to someone." I wince at my wild ideas, poking at my food. "Maybe I should start writing love letters to imaginary suitors to complete the picture."

Rob looks up at me with his big eyes, and I swear I can feel him judging me.

"What? Don't give me that look, Rob. You're the one eating off my plate," I say, defending myself against his silent disapproval.

I take a bite of my food and chew thoughtfully. I know exactly what I need: some wine and that awesome hot tub on the back screened-in porch.

After wrapping up dinner and putting the leftovers in the fridge, I go to my bedroom and pull out the black bikini I brought. I haven't even considered getting in until now, but I turned it on earlier, and if the roads are cleared tomorrow, this might be my last chance.

After tying my hair up into a messy bun, I slip into the hot water. My skin tingles as I sink deeper into the bubbles, enjoying the sensation of the warm jets massaging my back. The cold wind blows, and I sigh, letting the contrast of the warm water envelop me. A glass of wine in hand, I try to relax, to forget the tension, the kiss, the burnt asparagus, and Kyler's sudden departure. The cabin is silent, save for the gentle hum of the hot tub.

Just as I am about to relax, the screen door creaks open and Kyler appears, a towel wrapped dangerously low around his hips. His muscular form illuminated by the moonlight takes my breath away. I try to appear unfazed, but he can sense my surprise.

"Hey. I didn't expect you out here," I say, pretending not to have just yelped at the sight of him. "I left food for you in the fridge," I chirp into the tense atmosphere.

"I'm not hungry right now," he replies with an unreadable expression on his face.

"Too bad you missed the culinary masterpiece that was burnt asparagus," I reply lightly.

"Mind if I join?" he asks without breaking eye contact.

"It's a free country," I answer tartly, looking away from him as nerves start taking hold of me again.

He smirks knowingly and leans close. "Close your eyes if you don't want to see me naked."

I raise an eyebrow suspiciously before slowly shutting my lids. When I open them back up, I gasp at what awaits me: Kyler standing in front of me wearing an incredibly tight pair of pink swim trunks with rubber ducks printed all over them. They look more like bikini briefs than actual swimming shorts.

My throat feels tight as I stammer, "Um...a-are you comfortable in those?"

Kyler grins sheepishly as he steps in and sinks down into the bubbling water. "No, but I didn't want to make you feel weird."

He must have gone looking for something to wear so as not to make me uncomfortable.

I manage to smile "Ah...well, welcome to the hot tub!" I gesture grandly at the night and its beauty, hoping he doesn't read my nervousness.

Rob decides to join the party, leaping into the water and swimming around with abandon.

"Great, now Puck the Menace is here," Kyler says.

"You're such a goofball, aren't you?' I tell Rob, scratching his ears." I scoop him up, aware of Kyler's eyes on me. "Enjoying the view?" I ask sarcastically as I exit the tub to wrap Rob in a towel and dry his fur.

Kyler smirks as he lounges back with a beer in his hand and watches me with a lazy grin on his face. "It's not the worst I've seen."

I sniff then pick Rob up, put him back in the living room, and shut the door. I glance over my shoulder to find Kyler still looking at me, only this time the mask is down and he looks as if he's conflicted.

I swallow. "Do you want anything from the kitchen?"

"Are you coming back?"

"Of course. You're good company," I say softly.

"Even if it was a mistake?" His voice sounds bitter.

Christmas Cupid

He means the kiss. I pretend I don't get it. "I'll get you a beer."

I grab him another beer from the kitchen, and when I come back, his head is back against the edge of the hot tub and his eyes are closed. I move to set the beer next to him, and he grabs my hand. His eyes open, the set of his chiseled jawline tense.

"Iris?"

"Yes," I say shakily.

"I want you so bad," he says quietly.

A jolt of electricity runs through me, and I breathe out. "Same."

"What are we going to do about it?"

It's now or never. We're here, in this beautiful place, and I feel connected to him. There's nothing wrong with taking a chance.

I lean in and brush my mouth against his. He responds immediately, his tongue parting my lips. I feel his hands slide down my back to my hips, pulling me in closer to him. His touch sends shivers down my spine, and I moan into his mouth. Without a moment's hesitation, I get in the water and straddle him, feeling his hardness beneath me. He groans, his hands gripping my hips tightly. Our lips meet in a passionate kiss, our tongues dancing together as we explore. He tastes my skin, drinking me in as he kisses my cheek, my ear, and down my neck. Shivers dance over my body as my hands cling to his strong shoulders.

"I can't resist you," I say as I grind against him, my wet bikini bottoms against his trunks. His hands trail up my body, cupping my breasts. I arch my back, pushing myself into his hands, wanting more.

He breaks the kiss, his gaze on mine as he slowly pulls my bikini top down, exposing my breasts to him.

"So beautiful," he whispers as he takes a nipple into his mouth, sucking and nipping at it until it's hard and sensitized. I moan, melting into him and throbbing with desire.

He gently moves me in the hot tub and flips me over, positioning himself behind me. I gaze out at the night sky, overwhelmed by the sensory details hitting me all at one. The beautiful night, the warm water, the feel of his big hands on the globes of my ass as he squeezes and kneads it. I spread my legs, giving him better access.

I lean forward, propping myself up on my elbows. He runs his tongue down from the small of my back to the edges of my bikini bottoms. He pulls them down, exposing me to the cool air. I freeze, suddenly feeling vulnerable.

He pauses, wrapping his arms around my middle as he whispers in my ear. "Do you want to stop?"

"Don't stop," I whisper, and he hums an approval as he lifts my knees up to a seat in the hot tub. He strokes his fingers over my center to find me already drenched. He bends me forward, his tongue sliding along my core until it finds my clit.

I moan, feeling needy as my hands grip the edge of the tub. He teases me, running his tongue over it while he gently pushes a finger inside of me. It feels so good, and I can feel myself getting wetter. He adds a second finger, stretching me and playing with my G-spot. He works me, pulling me closer to the edge.

He removes his fingers, and I hear him discarding his trunks.

"Iris..." There's a question in the hoarse words.

"Yes," I plead.

My body trembles with anticipation as he pulls me against him. He grips my hips and pushes himself inside of me, stopping only to let me adjust to his size. Each thrust stirs up a tempest in my veins. He groans as he presses a kiss to my shoulder.

My breath catches in my throat as I vibrate with need. I can feel him within me, filling me. He pulls out, slowly, and then pushes back in. My body pulses against his, and I can feel my orgasm building almost immediately. He moves faster, and I push back, faster and faster, the slap of our bodies the only thing I hear.

He flips me over, his eyes darker than ever before, and we switch places. With a firm grip on my hips, he guides me, faster and faster until my body hums. He maneuvers me up and down, helping me work my body against his. I lean back as he traces his hands up my thighs, cupping my breasts in his hands. He massages them then gives a little pinch to my hard nipples. He reaches his hand back up to my neck, pulling me to his mouth for a passionate kiss.

I grab hold of his shoulders, using them for leverage. I thrust down onto him, his cock hitting the back of my pussy. He groans, and I can feel him getting harder inside of me.

I lean forward, kissing him. I move quickly until I can feel myself spiraling out of control. I moan into his mouth, my body bucking against his. My orgasm crashes over me, tightening my thighs and my stomach. I can feel myself gushing wetly around his thickness, my body clenching around him.

He groans as he calls out my name, holding me steady

as he thrusts up into me and climaxes. His mouth searches for mine and we kiss wildly, our tongues tangling.

He stops moving, his cock throbbing inside me. I shiver, trembling from the aftereffects.

Breathing heavily, he cups my face and gazes into my eyes. "Jesus, Iris, that... I didn't even use a condom." Worry flashes on his face as he presses his forehead to mine. "I'm sorry. It's just..."

My breathing still hasn't settled, and my words come out shakily. "There wasn't time. I'm on the pill anyway."

A half-smile curls his lips. "I didn't think I would be able to last."

I lean my head against his chest, listening to the comforting thump within it.

He tips my chin up. "Hey. No regrets, right?"

"Absolutely none." It was hot. It was crazy. He literally consumed me.

"Do you want to do it again?" he asks with a sheepish expression on his face. "It's, um, been a while for me."

"Now?"

He grins. "We can wait a few minutes."

I giggle. "Maybe inside this time, yeah? I can only imagine our neighbors out there watching us with binoculars."

He smirks, his brown eyes twinkling. "I guess we gave them a show."

Rob barks, and I look over at him. He has his nose pressed against the window part of the door. "He's the one that got a show."

"He isn't coming in the bedroom."

"Fine, but you better keep me warm tonight because

it's cold in there."

"Brat, I'll keep you warm all right." He sweeps me up as if I weigh nothing and gets out of the hot tub.

My body tingles with pleasure as I race to put on dry clothes, a pair of leggings and an oversized Vandy shirt. I marvel at myself in the mirror, my face glowing. I quickly apply some lip balm. When I return to the living room, Kyler has built a blazing fire in the fireplace. His hair is wet with droplets of water, and his muscles strain against his jeans as he tosses another log onto the flames.

My heart pounds fiercely at the sight of him. *Keep it together.* I clear my throat. "Are you hungry now?"

He waggles his eyebrows suggestively. "I did burn some calories."

"Great. I'll make you a plate."

"You don't have to. I can do it."

"I want to."

His face softens as he grabs me gently by the hand and brings it to his lips, grazing my knuckles softly with his mouth. "You're beautiful, Iris."

My heart thrums like a drumbeat, and I stifle a moan of desire then laugh. "Okay, okay, you're just sweet-talking me for extra salmon."

His eyes glimmer darkly as he pulls me close to him. His voice is husky with passion when he whispers, "I don't need to sweet-talk you. You've already given me everything I want, an amazing experience." His lips cover mine hungrily as if he can't get enough of me.

After Kyler finishes his meal, we curl up on the couch together to watch the mesmerizing flames. I feel peace inside me.

"So, what's on your Christmas list besides getting your hand back ready to play?"

He hums a little as he thinks. "Winning the Cup for sure, but hopefully when I'm on the ice. What about you?"

I sigh as I lean against him. "Just a better year, you know. I want to be happy. Also, I wouldn't mind taking a ride on the Ferris wheel I saw it town. I really loved the little village." A small laugh escapes my lips. "I might even come back here someday."

"Are you happy right now?"

I blush. "Um, yeah."

He twirls a piece of my hair. "You know, we don't have to do anything else. We can just be with each other and relax."

I nearly break my neck to look at him square in the eye. "Hey, it's been a while for me too, like over a year. We are so doing this."

He laughs, and I notice how his eyes crinkle in the corners. So sexy.

With a wicked glint in his gaze, he grabs my hand and leads me to the rug. He eases me effortlessly onto my back, and I gasp as he pins my arms above my head. His lips crash into mine, kissing me passionately as his hand slips up under my shirt, cupping my breast and making me moan against his mouth.

I'm already writhing with desire, so when he pulls away, I feel lost and exposed. But then he takes off his shirt and reveals his toned chest, and I greedily run my hands over him, exploring every inch of his perfectly sculpted chest.

While I whip off my sweatshirt, he slides his fingers

Christmas Cupid

under the waistband of my leggings and panties, tugging them down with one swift movement. I can barely catch my breath as I lie there before him, completely vulnerable yet filled with desperate longing.

Kyler smirks knowingly as he looks at me lying there beneath him. Then he takes his time, starting with teasing kisses that trail from my neck down to my breasts to my hipbone and all the way to my center. My pulse quickens as I feel his tongue slip inside me, driving me wild with pleasure. His hands firmly grip my legs and spread them farther apart so he can explore, pushing me closer to bliss with each intensifying lick of his talented tongue.

Arousal fills every molecule of my being until it feels like an explosion is about to erupt out of me. "Kyler," I moan, not able to take it anymore. "Don't stop."

He laps hungrily at my clit until I'm shaking uncontrollably in pleasure. He inserts two fingers and pumps them. I cry out as my orgasm comes crashing over me, my toes curling as sharp, indescribable pleasure shoots through me, pleasure so intense it's almost pain. My heart careens around in my chest like a drunken butterfly.

He pulls away from me.

I blink my eyes open. "What's wrong?"

He grins. "Why don't you come over here and find out?"

His voice is husky, his eyes dark. With the flames of the fire warming us, he peels off his jeans as I crawl over to him. He seems to like the way I crawl if that gleam in his gaze is anything to judge by. I look at his shaft. He's bigger than I thought he'd be, and my hands wrap around it as I stroke him, the velvety skin soft beneath my fingers.

He lies flat on his back, and I climb over him, straddling him. I put my arms around his neck and kiss his lips as I lower myself onto his cock. I gasp at the feeling of being so filled with him. He takes my hips and lifts them, angling my pussy so he can enter me more deeply.

"Kyler," I moan.

"Keep saying my name, sweetheart."

I repeat it over and over as I begin to move, slowly at first. He lets go of my hips and begins to massage my breasts, flipping my nipples expertly between his fingers. The combination of his shaft inside me and his fingers on my breasts is almost more than I can bear.

I kiss him harder, sucking his tongue as my pace quickens. I'm going to come again. I'm so close.

"Kyler," I whisper as I let go and fall into a hot spiral of pleasure. My body trembles and my neck arches up as I ride out the sensation.

"Iris!" I feel his body tense beneath me, and then his fingers dig into my hips as he rides out his own climax. He reaches up and holds me tight, his breath ragged in my ear. "Sweetheart."

I collapse on top of him and breathe in his warm male scent. The fire crackles next to us. The tree twinkles with lights. I have no clue where Rob went, but I'm glad he's quiet. Total bliss.

I must have said it aloud because he kisses my hair. "Total bliss."

* * *

This time, I really *was* having the best dream. I was in Kyler's arms, content for the first time in who knows how long. I could let my guard down without worrying about him using my heart for target practice. Also, there wasn't any fringe in sight.

When my eyes blink open, I smile sleepily, wishing I could wake up like this every morning. I gaze out the window, squinting against the blinding rays of sun that make their way through the thin curtains. I feel its warmth on my skin, and when I look outside, I see it's already starting to melt the snow from the evergreen branches.

I remember why I'm cuddled up in this cozy spot: Kyler. I turn to him, my breath hitching as I realize it's not a dream. The former object of hate is tangled in the sheets with me, his arm curled around me, his body against mine.

I sit up, careful not to wake him, taking in eyefuls of his body. His tanned skin contrasts with the white sheets. The dip and curve of every muscle, his strong chin, the long lashes most girls would kill for. I trace the lines of his pectoral muscles, right down to his navel, thinking of last night. The way his body was perfectly in sync with mine, the way we...

It almost feels like a sin to tear my eyes away, but I manage to. I slip out of bed, go to the bathroom, brush my hair and teeth, and stare at myself in the mirror. He has all those fans, can have any woman he wants, and yet he chose me.

Well, you were the only one available at the time.

Pushing that thought away, I slip into my furry robe and jump when I find him just sitting up in bed, a sleepy look in his eyes. He yawns and his eyes fall on me, making my heart somersault in my chest. "Hey. You getting up?"

I nod. "I was going to make breakfast."

He grabs his phone and checks the time. "Good idea. I'm starved. Need some help?"

"No." A weird feeling swirls in my stomach. I can't tell if it's a good or bad sick, though. Not yet. Yes, last night was incredible.

But...

What's next?

"Okay!" I say, way more chipper than I usually am. "Just give me a few!"

I sail out of the room, thinking, *That wasn't too awkward.*

In the kitchen, I crack eggs into a bowl, overthinking everything. All of last night. Every single word he said to me. All the times he told me how beautiful I am or how much he wanted me. It's enough to make goose bumps multiply on my skin, making me shiver.

I'm so deep in thought I don't realize he's crept up behind me until I feel his presence, like electricity zinging between us, even though he doesn't actually touch me. "What are you making?"

I jump a little. "Pancakes?"

Why am I so nervous around him? Ugh, the brave woman from last night is hiding.

"Love them. It reminds me of my mom. Are you sure I can't help?" He's so close I can feel his warm breath fanning my cheek.

I control myself, even when he brushes my hair aside and kisses my nape.

"I'm sure. You just sit. I love to cook."

He pours himself a cup of coffee then pads over to the table, wearing just his jeans. He slips into the chair, just as casual as can be. I crack an egg, and my fingers shake so much I get a bunch of shell pieces in the bowl. I try to fish them out, but they keep slipping away from my fingertip. "Ugh."

He probably thinks I'm a moron. "You were better at that yesterday."

Hmm. So I was. I can't wonder what's changed because *everything* has changed.

"Smells good."

I turn to gaze at him then stop myself. I don't need to make myself even more nervous by looking at him. "I haven't even started cooking yet."

I venture a look as I reach down to grab a pan, using my hair as a veil to hide, and see him watching me, a hungry look on his face. Does that mean he doesn't think last night was a colossal mistake?

I straighten, bowl in hand, and add the flour then stir—too hard. Powder fluffs out everywhere into my hair.

I sigh and glance over at him. How can he be that relaxed? And why is it that I'm a bumbling idiot? At least he doesn't notice.

"Hey, you okay?" he asks.

Okay, he notices.

Discretely wiping the flour from my front, I murmur, "Oh, yeah. Never better."

He cocks an eyebrow. "You sure?"

"A hundred percent." I'm looking at my stash of food and realizing I forgot syrup.

I suck.

He pushes away from the table, manspreading on the chair. He hooks a finger at me, gazing at me in a way that makes fresh need bloom deep inside me. "Come here, Iris."

I gaze at him. "Why? I need to—"

"Later," he promises, heat in his brown eyes.

He's very convincing. I step over to him, and his arms snake around my middle, pulling me toward him. I know where this will head if I let him have his way.

"Kyler? I don't know if—"

He stops and stares at me. "If what?"

My lips quiver as I struggle to form the words.

"If us having sex was okay?" he says softly.

I slowly nod. Despite all the pleasure it brought, the unknown pricks at me. I'm not a one-night stand kind of girl. My heart always gets involved, and I can't take another heartache. "I'm just processing it."

"Maybe you think too much. Just let your guard down."

Let my guard down? Doesn't he know there's a wall around my heart, especially this time of the year? "I can't."

His face tightens, and he releases me as he stands, putting distance between us. "No, I get it. It's not just because of your ex or your brother, right? I saw it in your eyes on New Year's. You and I together is..." He stops, his jaw popping. "Just a bit of cabin fever, yeah?"

"Wait, no. You can't count New Year's—I was fresh out of a breakup."

"You're making excuses." A huff comes from him as he puts his hands on his hips and paces around the room. "I should expect nothing less from a spoiled princess."

His words hurt.

"Wait," I try again, but he's already heading down the hall.

"The snowplows came through already," he mutters. "I've got to go, anyway. My flight's tomorrow and I haven't packed."

My hands fist. "I'm going to my mom's tomorrow, but we have time to eat breakfast. And talk."

He ignores me as he stalks to the bathroom and grabs his leather bag of soap and shampoo.

My throat tightens. He's jetting. He's *really* jetting. Rob follows him around in a daze, yipping as if trying to voice the thoughts storming around inside my brain.

Then my dog looks at me. *Mom, you're not just going to let him go, are you?*

No. Yes. I don't know!

Kyler comes back from the bedroom a second later, all dressed, grabbing his keys from the pocket of his jeans. I stare at the stuff around me. The tree we put up together. The decorations. Not having anyone to share this with is the least of my worries. He's just leaving. He's not even looking at me, or near me, at all.

When he does stop, I let out a sigh of relief. His voice is gruff. "Do you need a ride back?"

I blink. I'd almost taken it for granted that we would ride home together. How stupid. We didn't come here together. Why should I think what happened last night has any chance of continuing once we step outside this cabin?

"No. It's fine. I'll get a car." I'm surprised at how aloof I make my voice sound.

"Fine."

"What about the tree? I'll need help taking it down." I'm grasping at straws.

His lips compress. "I'll reimburse the owners for the extra work it might cause. I'll get their payment details from Will."

He goes to open the door, but Rob lunges and grabs his pant leg in his teeth, growling ferociously, trying to get him to stay.

"Rob," I whisper. I don't expect him to listen to me since he never does, but this time, he whimpers and comes back to me, sitting at my feet. Too bad, because I kind of wanted him to fight. *Someone* should be fighting, and yet I can't speak. I'm terrified of putting my heart on the line.

When the door is open, I hear the dripping of the melting snow, the singing of birds in the trees, and my gut tangles. This isn't like Liam all over again. No, this is worse. Because *Kyler*. There's a real connection here, well for me anyway. But if he's running off so fast, maybe that's what he wants and he's just using my uneasiness as an excuse.

He heads out the door, stooping a little so he doesn't bang the transom with his head, and my heart twists.

But then he turns, and his eyes fasten on me. He must feel the same as me, right? He doesn't want to leave.

Say it, I think. *Someone say it.*

He comes back in, and at first, I think he's bridging the distance to pull me into his arms and ask to spend Christmas with me. But then he walks by, opens the pantry door, and pulls out the bag with his leftover liquor.

This time when he leaves, he doesn't look back.

Chapter 16

Kyler

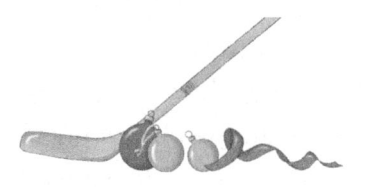

"Woohoo! Let's get this party started!"

If there's one person who knows how to live the rock-star life, it's the Predators' left wing, "The Wizard" Gibson. It's a good thing the man is a pro hockey player and was just signed to a sweet three-year contract with the organization. The way he spends money, he needs all the help he can get.

Case in point: this stretch limo. He rides in style everywhere he goes. His regular ride is a tricked-out, bright yellow Maclaren sportscar that announces he's coming from miles away.

Gibson is a good guy—my best friend, next to Will. The thing with him, though, is that he takes nothing seriously. The game, his lifestyle, none of it. He bounces through life as if in a mad fever dream. I have no idea if he worries about anything, or if he is even capable of worrying —his life is one big party. The fans respond to his carefree, outrageous behavior, and the organization knows he fills seats. He has more merch in the gift shop at the rink than any of us, most with the tagline "Off to see the Wizard!"

He wraps an arm around my neck and pulls me in close, delivering a wet, sloppy kiss to the top of my head. "We're going to get wasted tonight! And I'm horny as hell. Those girls down in Cabo had better be ready!"

There was a time when I lived to party. When he invited me on this trip, three months ago, I was all in. I liked the idea of sun and sand with my mistletoe. Tanned, bikini-wearing girls wouldn't hurt, either.

But now I just want the snow.

No, I want something else. Something...

"Dude, you all right?" Gibson says, lowering his sunglasses to look at me. His eyes are bloodshot—he always lives it up during our breaks. "You look like your dog died."

"I'm good." I yawn. "Just tired."

"Well, you'd better catch some Zs on the plane because we're going to be up all night!" He claps me on the back.

I doubt I'll be able to rest on this flight. The six of us will be taking up much of first class, but I guarantee the rest of the cabin is going to hate us, especially if none of them like hockey. Even if they do, once they get a taste of Gibson's antics, they might start rooting for the other team.

"Hey, how was your trip? Slappy said you were taking some days in the mountains," Carrel, a second-string center, says to me as he sips his whisky.

"It was..." It should've been terrible, but now that I think about it, it was far better than that. As I stopped at the post office to mail the earrings to my nieces, I realized it wasn't nearly what I expected. It was so much better—but I can't tell them that. "Fine."

"Sounds boring to me," Gibson says with a smirk. Of course he'd think that. No party equals no fun. "You see any of that snow?"

"Yeah. A little."

The second we get to Nashville International, he jumps out of the limo, already turning heads since he's holding his trademark Gandalf walking stick. When he's not carrying his hockey stick, he's sure to have this one in his grasp.

"The Wizard!" people start to shriek and whisper around us.

This is him, in all his glory. He's smiling at the women, high-fiving the businessmen late for their flights, hip-checking the porters, giving candy canes to the little kids, all while shouting to everyone and anyone that he's going on vacation. The rest of us get out and stand by our luggage, watching the show.

"Odds are ten to one we get kicked off the plane," says Briggs, one of our defensemen.

Another defenseman nods. "If not the plane, then definitely the hotel."

I grimace. They're right. We got kicked out of a hotel once, and at the time, I didn't care. I was twenty-two, new to the team, and loved every second of the party animal life. I slept on the beach, drunk out of my mind, half-clothed, with two girls, one under each arm.

But right now, all I can do is think of the woman I had tucked under my arm this morning. I remember how she felt under my hands, the silkiness of her skin, the softness of her hair, the glint in her green eyes that told me she wanted me.

My heart twinges. I want to go back to that cabin. I want to have a redo where I keep my ass in the kitchen chair, and we talk just like she wanted. A long exhale comes from my chest. Instead, I ran. I got scared and freaked out and took it out on her.

Right now, she's probably on the way to her mother's house. She and Will and her mom are going to have that amazing, old-fashioned family Christmas with a big tree, great homemade food, gifts, badly sung carols, the works.

And I'm going to have...The Wizard.

I look over at him as I grab my suitcase and wheel it toward check-in. He's standing on the thing meant to weigh luggage, saying, "You shall not pass," to the girl at the counter as he hands over his passport. I don't know why this grates on me.

Yes, I do, actually.

It's fine. After all the peace and quiet, this is just a change of pace. I need a few hours to get back into the swing of things. By the end of this week, I'll be back to my old self. Right where I was...

Before. And I want to do that again...why?

I look down at my hand. Yeah, I can keep playing, tell my agent and the doctors to screw off, or I can man up and accept what I need to do.

I'm long due. Maybe if I hadn't been such an idiot, if I'd opened my mouth and told her I didn't want to leave... maybe she and I would be having that Christmas together.

She'll probably kick my ass to the curb, but I won't know unless I try. Like Gretzky said, you miss all the shots you don't take. And even if she does kick me out, at least it's better than not knowing what could've been, right?

Christmas Cupid

We're in the long security line, people in front of and behind us. Gibson is stopping every once in a while to sign an autograph.

I look back at the exit. This is my last chance. If I'm going to do it, I have to do it now.

Gibson looks at me. "Dude, you forget something?"

"No, I just remembered something," I say, handing him my ticket. "I'm not in college anymore."

His eyes narrow. "What?"

"I can't go. I have something I have to do." I hoist my bag onto my shoulder and prepare to break through the line.

He lays a hand on my shoulder. At first, I think he might try to convince me to stay. Instead, he says, "All we have to decide is what to do with the time that is given us."

I stare. That's a Gandalf quote, isn't it? "What does that mean?"

He nods like some wise sage. "Death is just another path, one we all must take."

"Is that Yoda now?" I shake my head. "Forget it. I'm out."

As I turn away and break through the line, headed for the exit, he calls, "Fine, be that way. More hotties for me!"

That's fine. I have my eye on just one.

Chapter 17

Iris

It smells like seafood and bayberry candle in the kitchen as I pour another glass of spiked eggnog and take a long swig.

"Whoa, easy on that, sis," Will says to me from my mother's old record player, where he's putting on Dean Martin's Christmas hits. "It has to last all night, and I don't want you sloshed before you open up the present I got you."

I roll my eyes. It's another tradition—my brother always gets me the ugliest Christmas pajamas known to man. Last year, it was llamas in Santa hats with neon UFOs. I think he has them specially made to be hideous. It's okay because I always buy him something with pickles. I don't even know how it started, just that every year, I get him pickles. He hates pickles. Sure, we could spend tons of money on expensive gifts, but somehow the silly gifts make it more meaningful. I smile to myself as I recall the pickle sweater I knitted for him a couple of years ago. This year I got him pickle vodka.

"I'm not sloshed," I say as he reaches for a bacon-wrapped scallop. "But you'd better save room for my gift."

He narrows his eyes at me and grabs another one, downing it in one bite.

"So...you never told me. How was your weekend?" he says, casual as ever.

He's fishing. That's fine. Yes, I called him to come pick me up yesterday instead of an Uber since there weren't any around because of the holidays, and I was quiet on the whole ride home. I don't know for sure if he tried to set me and Kyler up, but I have a feeling he did. He'd never admit to it directly, so I've decided to play like nothing happened and have *him* be the one who brings it up.

"It was fine. Like I told you, the cabin wasn't as nice as the pictures. The bedroom was quite cold. Poor Rob shivered even under the covers."

"Huh. Interesting. You got cold with that fireplace? Do you even know how to build a fire?"

"Yep," I say as I sit down at the kitchen table and pile Rob into my lap. That is if you count watching Kyler build one. "The heat in the bedroom sucked. I had to sleep in front of the fire." I feed Rob a bit of bacon. "Didn't we, Mr. Robby-bunkins?"

Rob yips.

Will pops some peanuts into his mouth. "What a hardship."

I ball up a napkin and chuck it at him. "Not to mention it snowed. A lot."

He smiles. "It's almost as if Santa knew you needed snow to complete the Christmas miracle. I saw that the porch area had been shoveled. How'd you dig yourself out?"

I'm so onto him. He's looking guiltier and guiltier. Normally, he wouldn't care. He's only asking this question because he knows I'd never shovel all that snow on my own. I had to have had help. He wants me to mention Kyler.

And I will not do it. I've decided to ban speaking of him from my life forevermore.

If only it were that easy.

I really thought I was wrong about Kyler; thought he was different. Yesterday on the entire ride home, while Will kept trying to get me to talk, I kept thinking of Kyler, so much so I nearly went mad. What I did wrong. What I could have said to keep him there. I went from the highest of highs the night before to the lowest of lows that morning. I couldn't stop wondering what I could have done to make for a different outcome.

But now that I'm here, talking to Will, who just got done telling Mom about the two girls he dated over the past few weeks—neither of whom have any sticking power—I know the answer.

Nothing.

My mother gave him the regular lecture—he's thirty, he only has a few more good years playing hockey, and he's going to want something else to give his life meaning after that. Will just stared at her like she was speaking a different language.

And Kyler is like Will and the rest of those hockey players. They mean well. They're good guys. And yet, when it comes to women, they have absolutely no idea what they want. The one thing they're sure they don't want: permanency.

So, to avoid saying anything about his friend, I just say, "There was a nice old couple there that helped dig us out."

"Us?" He sees the opening.

I pet my dog. "Rob and me."

His face falls. That's not the answer he wanted.

I threw myself into the cleaning after Kyler left. I practically worked my fingers to the bone trying to scrub away any thoughts of him. "I cleaned it too, left it even better than when I got there. Per your instructions."

He frowns. "So...what'd you do up there, alone, in the snow?"

"A little bit of everything. Cooking, making some crafts, drinking a little wine..." I haven't fibbed once. "You should have seen me chopping that tree and decorating it."

"Huh." He's frustrated, gnawing on the inside of his cheek. And that's when I know.

He did this on purpose.

The thing is, though, Will? You may be the golden boy, may be used to getting everything you want at a snap of your fingers, but the real world is messy. Some things don't work out the way you want them to, no matter how hard you try.

I'm about to tell him that when my mother claps her hands. "Dinner is ready!"

She brings over this giant pot of spaghetti with shrimp

and clam sauce, and Will licks his lips. "Wow, Mom. You outdid yourself."

I smile, trying to enjoy this. I missed this last year. I need to be present in this moment, need to fully enjoy my family.

And yet...

Will pours us each a glass of wine and then holds his up. "First, to start this celebration, what should have been our twenty-seventh annual Christmas together but is just our twenty-sixth, because of *someone* who shall remain nameless..." He mock glares at me. "I got our prodigal family member a special gift that she must open right now."

I glance at the poorly wrapped, over-taped package he hands me, eyes narrowing. I know what this is. Reluctantly grabbing it, I pull it open to find a reindeer onesie complete with felt antlers and a red nose.

"You have to put it on."

I glare at him then look at my mom, who nods. And here I thought they were sympathetic to me. I laugh.

"Put. It. On. Put. It. On," they chant as I stand up and slip it over my leggings and sweater.

I zip it up and spin for them. "Happy?"

"Hood, too."

I flip the hood up. I know I must look ridiculous when they both burst out into laughter.

"Let's eat," I declare, sitting down.

We dig into the food with Dean Martin's "Marshmallow World" playing in the background. We tease Mom about her gift (a trip to Italy—she's always wanted to go) and joke about how we should have an album of us singing Christmas tunes since we're so good at it. It's perfect.

Then Will gets a text and looks down at it. He snorts and looks at me. "So, when were you going to tell me what really happened this weekend?"

I frown. "What do you mean?"

When he looks down at his phone, I try to glance at the display, but he snatches it away.

I grip my fork in my hand and aim it at him. "Who is that? What did he say?"

He gives me a mysterious waggle of his eyebrows. "Wouldn't you like to know?"

I lunge for him with the fork, trying to grab the phone out of his hand. He holds it up, and his arms are so gorilla-long I can't reach. He jumps up and I follow, rounding the table to confront him. I reach for the phone again, but he snatches my reindeer hood, pulling me back.

My mother tries to get us to stop, first gently, then more insistently, but before long, somehow—I don't know how—some of the food gets involved as I toss a few strings of linguine at Will.

"Stop it right now!" Mom yells, and we both come to our senses at once and look at ourselves. We're both red-faced and breathing hard. "When are you two going to stop acting like kids around each other?"

We cast death glares across the table.

Then a second later, it dissolves into maniacal laughter. My mother just watches, perplexed, as I pick a strand of linguine from the collar of his shirt and pat his cheek.

Mom sighs. "You two are idiots."

"Sorry, Mom," Will says, jumping up and starting to retrieve some bits of pasta off the ground.

Luckily, we haven't made too much of a mess, but as I start to help him, I realize he left his phone on the table. I pick it up and see a message from Kyler. My heart skips at the name, but then I read it.

It's not about me.

Just wanted to let you know I had a meeting with the doc, and I need the surgery. I'm out for the season. Sorry man.

I look up to find Will staring at me, gauging my reaction. I shrug. "Oh, that's all? Why were you hiding that from me?"

He smirks. "Just because."

Because he likes to rile me up, that's why. "You must be pissed. Isn't he one of your right-hand men?"

He gives me a look, silent, assessing, and I know what he's thinking. *You know he is.* But I continue to play innocent, waiting for a response.

Finally, he just says, "Yep, but there's always next year," and goes to the trash to throw away the result of our food fight.

My mother looks at me. "What was that all about?"

I sit down in the chair and pull my hood up. It's actually a blessing—this floppy hood with the Rudolph nose covers most of my face. "Nothing."

"It's got to be something. I've never seen you so worked up."

I sigh, about to tell her it's nothing again, when I look up into the doorway and see Will standing there, looking smug as ever. "Look what I found when I was taking out the trash."

It's Kyler. He's wearing a black hoodie and joggers with a Preds hat over his unruly hair. He still hasn't shaved. His eyes lock on mine and my heart speeds up in my chest, hammering so hard I lose my breath.

But my feet know exactly what to do. Before my head can get with the picture, I'm up on my feet, rushing toward him.

"Aren't you supposed to be on a plane to Cabo?"

"I had a change in plans."

"Oh. Why?"

My eyes shift between him and my brother. Neither says a word, but they're both looking at me.

"You," Kyler says gently. "You're the reason."

Behind me, Mom says, "What's going on here?"

"Give us a minute," I say as I grab Kyler by the hand and walk him down the hall and out to the front porch.

"Nice outfit," he says, smiling.

I brush a piece of linguine off my front, as if that makes me look any better. Then I shove back my hood and say, "I didn't expect to see you."

"I couldn't go."

"You couldn't...I see that."

He looks back toward the house, where my brother is standing by the lit window, badly pretending he isn't spying on us through the hole of the wreath there. "I'm sorry if I ruined your holiday by being here."

I stare at him, incredulous. He's only made it better. "Of course you didn't. But—"

"I shouldn't have left you like that, in the middle of our Christmas. It was wrong. I was a coward and all I could think about on the way home was us decorating the tree and that moment when you fell into my arms." He lowers his lashes. "And the sex, I thought about that a whole lot."

"Oh."

He adjusts his hat, almost nervously. "I expected the cabin visit to be the worst, most depressing weekend of my life, especially when you showed up. But it wasn't. Not at all. Instead, everything was...really good. You asked me what I'd want on my Christmas list, and it would be you and me...seeing if this is real."

My heart soars. Oh, it's real, and he's so cute as he talks. It's adorable, and sweet, and I want to pull him to me, right now.

He has more to say. "You made me realize what I'm missing in my life: someone who gets me. Yeah, we seem to be opposites, but we aren't. You love to cook, and I like to watch you. You're bratty and I adore it. I'm a hockey player, but really, I think you respect the game. You get it. You know how hard I work and how much my injury drives me nuts."

I glance at his hand. "I do."

"We both lost some of our love for the holidays because of our pasts, but I like to think spending time with you in the cabin has brought so many feelings of, shit, I don't know, love back into my life. Yeah, it snowed a lot, and we argued a lot, but I wouldn't change any of it." He scuffs at the ground in his sneakers. "I *like* bickering with you."

I can't speak. All I can get out is "Ah."

Christmas Cupid

I can tell that was not exactly the answer he was hoping for. Then he says, "Well, now that I got that off my chest, Merry Christmas. Do you want me to go?"

"Are you crazy?" I reach over and grab his shoulder, pulling him toward me. Tilting my head, I gaze up at him. "I'm not letting you go again. You're staying. But I warn you—it can get pretty crazy. You're either in, or you're out. You understand?"

His grins. "So do I get pajamas, too?"

"Absolutely. I'm going to find some of Will's old ones for you." He leans down to kiss me, but I know Will's watching, so I take his hand. "Come on."

"Where are we going?"

"You'll see." I pull open the front door and run inside, past the kitchen and dining room where my family is waiting. My little pup, catching the hint, bounds up too as I practically drag Kyler up the stairs to the loft room.

My old bedroom.

When we get in there and I turn around, he's already grinning. "Good to know it didn't go to waste."

I smile up at the giant Christmas tree. Will and I had a hard time dragging it into the bed of the truck, as big as it was. I had to decorate it with my own stash of ornaments this time, and that makes it even more beautiful. But it's not quite done.

As I grab the star from the box, my funny little dog yips excitedly. "Shh, Puck," I whisper to him.

"Puck?" Kyler asks, amused.

"What can I say? The name's grown on me." I hold up the star. "Give me a boost?"

He nods and stoops, allowing me to climb onto his broad shoulders. As I rise up, a sense of familiarity envelops us, a feeling of unity and synchrony as if we've done this a thousand times before. I gently place the star on the top of the tree, and we remain steady, unwavering.

"That's it," I whisper, my voice a soft murmur in the silence of the room.

He lowers me down gently, our eyes locking, our breaths mingling in the space between us, creating an invisible thread connecting our souls. His arms are strong around me, and I can't help but lose myself in his gaze.

A weekend ago, the thought of this man, this formidable hockey Beast, making me feel such overwhelming happiness and vibrant aliveness would have been unimaginable. But here we are, and the joy radiating through me is palpable. I know, deep in my heart, this is just the beginning of something beautiful, something magical.

A shiver runs through me, a mixture of excitement and emotion, forcing me to break our gaze and look at the tree. That's when I notice something amiss. It's not quite perfect.

"Oh. The star isn't—"

Before I can finish, he takes my chin in his big, warm hand, turning my face toward his, and captures my mouth with his own. His kiss is a symphony of emotions, a promise of love, and a reminder of our journey.

In this moment, as his lips move against mine, I realize while nothing in life is perfect, some things, some moments, are infinitely better, more beautiful, more precious. They are the moments that make life worth living, the times that bring light to the darkness, and I'm grateful, so incredibly grateful, to have found this moment with him.

* * *

Dear Reader,

Thank you for reading *Christmas Cupid*. I hope you enjoyed Kyler and Iris's story as much as I did. If you want more contemporary romance featuring pro athletes, check out my next full length novel that is releasing December 2023: My Darling Bride. As an added bonus you can read a sneak peek excerpt from My Darling Bride starting after this note.

Reviews are like gold to authors, and I read each and every one. If you have a few moments, please consider leaving a rating or a review for Christmas Cupid.

Keep reading all the books.

XOXO,
Ilsa

. . .

P.S. Sign up for my newsletter below and you will receive a FREE Briarwood Academy novella just for joining.

http://www.ilsamaddenmills.com/contact

Please join my FB readers group, Unicorn Girls, to get the latest scoop as well as talk about books, wine, and Netflix:

https://www.facebook.com/groups/ilsasunicorngirls/

Bonus Excerpt from My Darling Bride

My Darling Bride

Copyright © 2023 by Ilsa Madden-Mills
Publisher: Montlake Publishing

EMMY

The hot Arizona sun, a pool, and a beverage. Sounds delightful, but the sun is a volcano, the pool belongs to a shithole place called the Golden Iguana, and my beverage is a tepid bottle of Fiji water.

There's one thing that makes me smile: the motel sign has a faded green-and-gold iguana on it, standing upright and grinning as he welcomes you with open arms. He reminds me of that insurance lizard. I've named him Darcy.

Welcome to Old Town, a small place outside Tucson

Bonus Excerpt from My Darling Bride

in the middle of the Sonoran Desert. A six-hour drive from Vegas, it seemed the last place Kian would look. Sure, I could have caught a plane back to New York, but I wasn't thinking straight when I left the Bellagio.

I cling to the edge of the pool as a Lamborghini with blacked-out windows roars into the parking lot, the engine growling like a beast. Low slung and shiny, the car is lemon yellow, the golden bull emblem sparkling in the sunlight. It parks next to a rusted pickup truck.

"I guess the Four Seasons was booked," I snark to myself, then wince at my raspy voice. My throat is swollen and aches horribly.

When no one gets out of the car right away, hair rises on the back of my neck.

Wait a minute . . . did Kian rent a different car and follow me?

Nah. He had a bachelor party last night, which means he's sleeping it off today; plus, I only grabbed a small bag of essentials when I left. My suitcase is still in the room at the Bellagio, along with most of my clothes. For all he knows, I'm wandering around the casinos, pissed at him.

Whatever. It doesn't matter. I'm overthinking it.

I'll never let you go, Emmy.

I push Kian's last words away as I sink underwater, swim to the ladder, and scramble up the steps. I gather my book and sunscreen, then adjust my hair around my shoulder, hiding the purple bruises on my neck. Sliding on my flip-flops, I'm dripping water as I make my way to the gate that leads to the rooms, keeping a wary eye on the car.

The driver's side door opens, and a dark-haired man gets out.

Bonus Excerpt from My Darling Bride

I'm not even aware of how relieved I am until my shoulders sag. Not Kian.

Stretching his arms up and rolling his neck, the man squints at the sun, swears under his breath, then reaches inside the car. His back is broad. Like, fucking big. He must be at least six and a half feet tall. He thrusts on a pair of aviators and glares at the iguana on the sign as if he's got a personal vendetta. I don't know what he has against Darcy.

Muttering a curse, he slams the car door, then shoves a ball cap over his hair. The hat casts his face in shadow, giving him a dark aura.

Lambo looks about as cuddly as a steak knife.

Dressed in designer jeans that cling to his thighs and an expensive-looking button-down with the cuffs rolled up, he has a blade for a nose, sculpted cheekbones, and sensuous lips. Tall. Broad. Muscled. Sex on a stick. Swipe right, ladies.

He takes long strides yet somehow manages to appear graceful—no, scratch that, athletic.

My guess? He's felt the crack of bone under his hands.

He exudes broodiness. My favorite.

I allow myself to picture just what kind of sexual damage he might cause, wondering at the thrill of being caught up in his arms when he unleashes.

Oh yeah. I'd ride that stallion like a cowgirl gone wild.

I mentally slap myself.

No. More. Men.

My next date will be with a rom-com and a kitten. A cat would be a superb boyfriend—hair balls but no drama.

As I'm picturing kittens dancing around a ball of yarn,

Lambo slings a duffel over his shoulder and heads to the front office.

Goodbye, sexy beast. Enjoy your stay at the crappiest motel in Arizona.

Hustling, I head in the opposite direction and take the rusted metal stairwell up to the third-floor-balcony breezeway that leads to my room.

"Hey, gorgeous," a voice murmurs from behind me, and I whip around in surprise to see Clint Eastwood—not the real one, but a cheap knockoff.

Fake Clint showed up in the motel honky-tonk bar last night in a legit black leather duster, boots, and a hat. He lurked in the shadows cast by the flashing neon lights while I drank at the bar. He made the rounds, chatting up every woman in the place, and I left before he got to me.

I glance around the empty breezeway as my unease rises higher. A knot forms in my gut, and my breathing quickens. I'm alone here. Best to not engage with Clint. I make a noncommittal sound and start to my door.

"Hey, wait, don't run off," he says as he follows on my heels. "I saw you at the pool. You were swimming laps like it was your job."

His eyes linger on my breasts, and I groan inwardly, regretting I didn't pull on a shirt. I'm in a black rash-guard shirt and bikini bottoms I bought from the dollar store in town.

"Thought I'd join you, maybe get a few laps in, but now you're done. Too bad." He holds up a longneck beer. "I've got more of these in my room if you want one?"

"I'm in for the day," I say as I rummage in my worn patchwork bag, searching for the motel key.

Bonus Excerpt from My Darling Bride

"You're alone here, right?"

My warning radar spikes. "No," I reply slowly. "My boyfriend is asleep in the room."

"I didn't see him last night."

"He doesn't like crowds. Or guys hitting on me."

"Hard to believe he'd let you drink alone." He stares at my navel ring peeking through my rash guard, then gives me a smarmy grin. "I noticed your room is next to mine. Talk about some cardboard walls. I heard you crying this morning. Did you have a fight with him?"

Play nice, the angel on my shoulder says, while the devil...

I find the motel key and grip it tight. "Should I wake up my boyfriend and tell him you're being a dick?"

"I like your spunk, but I'm just trying to get to know you. No need to involve your man. If that's even true." He eases around me until he's blocking my door.

His bloodshot hazel eyes hold mine. He's older than my twenty-eight and reeks of beer. Today he's wearing cutoff shorts, a faded shirt, and flip-flops. I guess the duster and boots were too hot for day attire. With a buzz haircut, a weak chin, and beady eyes, he looks like a mean hamster. And now I'm picturing a hamster in a cowboy outfit riding a horse in the desert and having a gunfight with Darcy the Iguana.

I'm five-nine and can hold my own, especially in heels, but he towers over me.

"Ease up. Just have a drink with me. I'm bored here. Where are you from?"

"Get out of my way, or my boyfriend will kick your ass."

"Yeah? What's his name?"

My brain scrambles for a name. "Darcy."

"Weird name." He touches a strand of my hair, and my heart thunders, part outrage, part fear.

Scenarios dance through my head. He's intoxicated. His door is currently open, and he's blocking me from mine. He could push me inside his. He could drag me. Flashbacks of my father dragging my mother burn inside my head.

The air thickens with tension. Sweat beads on my upper lip as my muscles quiver with the instinct to flee.

The sounds of footsteps arrive on the walkway, and relief hits like a tidal wave.

Lambo strides our way as he tucks his sunglasses into the pocket of his shirt. He seems to weave on his feet, then rightens himself by clinging to the balcony rail. His head turns to us, and he pauses, his eyes tightening, flicking from me to Fake Clint.

"What's going on?" he asks, his tone a dark velvet rumble.

Fake Clint takes a step back and holds his hands up in a placating manner. "I'm just on my way to the pool. You checking in?"

Lambo ignores him and comes back to me, his face expressionless. "You all right?"

It's as if I've manifested him. Give the man a cravat, and he's Darcy! As in, the guy from Pride and Prejudice, not the iguana. Well, him too.

A surge of adrenaline hits. Pasting on my brightest smile, I drop my bag and rush forward and wrap my arms around his waist in a bear hug. He grunts as we collide, his body a solid wall of hard muscle. My head hits him midchest. Oh, he must work out twenty-four seven, and kill me now, but he smells intoxicating, like dark cherries, expensive leather, and cedar.

My head tilts back as my eyes implore him, hoping he catches on quick. Swallowing down the pain in my throat, I manage to say the words in a husky (hopefully sexy) voice. "It's okay, honey bunny, he didn't mean anything. Honest. No reason to get upset—you don't want to violate your parole. I know how jealous you get. Remember in Chicago, when you beat that man to a pulp for dancing with me? We can't repeat that. It was carnage."

"What? I don't—" he starts.

"Oops, I shouldn't have brought that up. You don't like me to talk about your time in prison. It was so hard to be away from each other. Your passionate letters were the only thing that kept me going." I stretch up on my tiptoes and brush my lips over his cheek. The scruff on his square jawline tickles my lips. "Don't worry, I told this guy I was taken."

His hand lands on my ass and tugs me closer—instinct, I suppose, when a woman claiming to know you throws herself in your direction.

END EXCERPT

***

If you would like to read the rest of Graham and Emmy's story grab your copy of My Darling Bride (Releases Dec

Bonus Excerpt from My Darling Bride

2023). It is a brand new, full length, standalone story, available only through Amazon.

Also by Ilsa Madden-Mills click here

About the Author

Wall Street Journal, New York Times, and *USA Today* bestselling author Ilsa Madden-Mills writes about strong heroines and sexy alpha males that sometimes you just want to slap. A former high school English teacher and elementary librarian, she adores all things *Pride and Prejudice*; Mr. Darcy is her ultimate hero. She loves unicorns, frothy coffee beverages, vampire books, and any book featuring sword-wielding females.

*Please join her FB readers group, Unicorn Girls, to get the latest scoop as well as talk about books, wine, and Netflix:

https://www.facebook.com/groups/ilsasunicorngirls/

You can also find Ilsa at these places:

Website:
http://www.ilsamaddenmills.com
News Letter:
http://www.ilsamaddenmills.com/contact

The End

Made in the USA
Las Vegas, NV
27 November 2024